Pastels

Ron Ranson's
PAINTING
SCHOOL

Pastels

DIANA CONSTANCE

BROCKHAMPTON PRESS
LONDON

First published in Great Britain in 1994 by
Anaya Publishers Ltd., Strode House,
44-50 Osnaburgh Street, London, NW1 3ND.

This edition published 1995 by Brockhampton Press,
a member of Hodder Headline PLC Group

Managing Editor: Helen Douglas-Cooper
Art Director: Jane Forster
Design Assistant: Sarah Willis
Photography: Diana Constance

British Library Cataloguing in Publication Data
Constance, Diana
Pastels. - (Ron Ranson's Painting School Series)
I. Title II. Series
741.2

ISBN 1 86019 181 9

Typeset in Great Britain by
Litho Link Ltd, Welshpool, Powys, Wales.
Colour reproduction by J. Film Process, Singapore
Printed and bound by Oriental Press, Dubai

Contents

Foreword   6

Introduction   8

THE BASICS

Materials   14

Colour   22

Tonal Values and Colour   28

Composition   34

Techniques   42

Frottage   50

THE ELEMENTS

Flowers   56

Textures   68

Sketchbook Work   76

Light   78

Space   86

Landscape   90

Sky and Weather   100

Assessing Your Work   112

Index   118

Useful addresses   120

Foreword

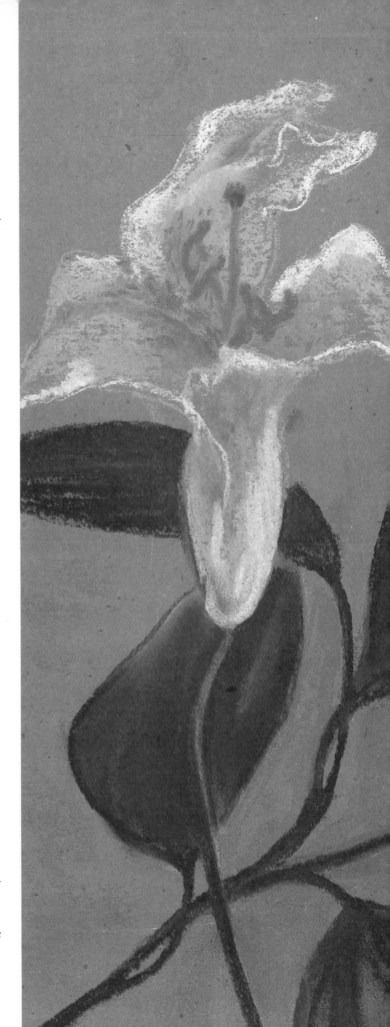

As many of you know, I am basically a watercolourist, and as Series Editor for this collection of books it's been a necessary pleasure to choose the work of other artists to illustrate the other media in the series. One of the distinguishing features of these artists has been their ability not only to excite and inspire, but also to teach, while retaining the individuality that marks their work as out of the ordinary.

Pastel itself has always been known as a fairly easy medium to use initially, but the difficulty has been to imbue it with strong individual style – Diana succeeds here magnificently.

A native New Yorker, her initial training was at the Art Students League – one of the most prestigious art schools in America. Later, New Mexico, probably the most exciting state in America from an artistic point of view, had an obvious influence on Diana's work, as did her five years in Rome. Is it any wonder that her style is not only exciting, but also has a truly international flavour, powerful in design and rich and strong in colour?

In this book, Diana shows how you can obtain rewarding results very quickly, so building enthusiasm and confidence in the reader.

For a complete beginner, pastel is probably the best way to get into art because you are immediately in touch with colour. You don't have to mix colours or squeeze out tubes, you just pick up the colour and put it on the paper in one go. However, for the more experienced artist, pastel provides great opportunities for real sophistication of approach. In other words, there's a whole lifetime of interest and growth in just this one medium.

Ron Ranson

The dark sinuous leaves of this flower are as important to the drawing as the flower itself, and the drawing was influenced by Japanese prints, which give equal value to all parts of a bloom, rather than centring attention on the showy flower. The leaves of this flower were pulled out and arranged before drawing it, and a pastel pencil was used for the stem and the outline of the leaves. The flowers were drawn with soft pastels. The paper was a coarse, recycled pastel paper.

Introduction

Pastels have had a rather chequered history. Leonardo da Vinci (1452-1519) was the first master known to have used them, although only to enliven some of his charcoal and sanguine sketches.

Pastel is regarded as a particularly French medium, and seems to have first been used extensively as a medium in its own right by Jean Perréal (1455-1530), a minor court artist to Louis XII. It was probably Perréal who first introduced Leonardo to it on a visit to Milan.

The real popularity of the medium didn't begin until the rich bourgeois culture of the Italian city states developed in the 16th century. No state was richer than Venice or had grander commissions for its artists. Jacopo Tintoretto (1518-94) and his followers quickly saw the possibilities for this versatile medium and began using it for the highlighting and skin tones in their cartoons for church commissions.

But it was a Venetian woman artist, Rosalba Carriera (1675–1757) who popularized the medium and particularly the female portrait. She inspired French 18th-century masters like Maurice Quentin de la Tour (1704-88), Jean-Baptiste Perronneau (1715-83) and, later in his career, Jean-Baptiste-Siméon Chardin (1699-1779) and the Swiss artist, Jean-Etienne Liotard (1702-89).

Their great 18th-century masterpieces were unfortunately followed by some of the most frivolous works in pastel, giving it a reputation as an ephemeral medium. Following the French Revolution the medium was condemned, along with its former clients, as the minor art form of a frivolous and now defunct class.

It might have languished had it not been for the dashing figure of Eugène Delacroix (1798-1863). His full-blooded yet sensitive pastels are not as well known as his oils. However, a few of them can still be seen in his atelier, preserved in Quatier Ste Germaine on the Left Bank in Paris.

Pastel's full rehabilitation came with Edgar Degas (1834-1917), who was a great admirer of the work of Delacroix. His eye and tireless innovations rescued pastels. The fascinating boulevardier life of late 19th-century Paris – on the streets and in the boudoir – found the perfect mode of expression in pastel. Degas could simulate the mundane yet titillating detail of a woman's toilette in his studio, working through long sessions with difficult poses, using sheets of heavy watercolour paper – layering, steaming, layering again with soft pastel. Thus he gave us sensual images of feminine intimacy that capture a time and mood with unequalled sensitivity that he could never have achieved with formal easel painting in oils.

Although pastel is a very different type of medium from oil paints, they share some basic techniques. Both rely on building up layers of pigment. In oil painting, a thin layer of diluted paint is used to block in the basic forms of the composition. In pastel

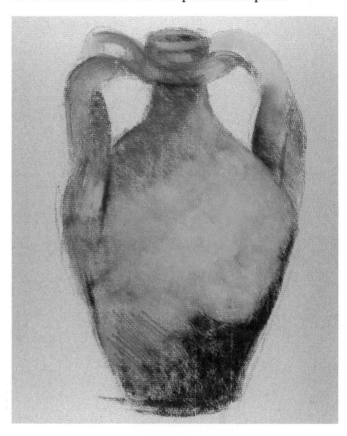

Above, one of the advantages of pastels is that they can be used in a very direct way and left unblended, relying on the interplay of warm and cool colours and light and dark tones to create the impression of form in an object.

Contrasts in texture between smoothly blended areas and distinctive, unblended marks are one of the unique qualities of pastels.

Pastels can be used in a variety of ways. It is possible to use them on wet paper to create a very soft, diffused effect. Hard or soft pastels can be used for this, and the marks spread because the paper is damp.

painting, the side of the stick is rubbed lightly over the paper to define the basic shapes. This is the first, light layer of pastel, over which subsequent layers are added. This layer can be left as it is and worked into, or slightly rubbed back or blended before the next layer of pastel is added.

Pastel is most effective when it is used to create an impression of a subject, instead of a literal, photographic representation. This is because, when we look out over the landscape, or even at a simple still life, our eyes are registering a great variety of information about the depth, weight, tone and colour of the shapes in the subject.

An artist tackles this mass of information by first sketching in the main shapes in the subject, creating a framework within which the painting can grow. With all the large areas roughed in, the artist can step back and judge the balance of the work as a whole. Some areas can be blended at this stage so that there is a good variety of textures in the work.

Each layer of pastel is applied over previous layers without smothering them, so that a rich tapestry of colour is woven. At the end of the work, line or detail is added. Certain areas are blended to create a good contrast in textures. If the painting has been done on a heavy watercolour paper that has a rough surface, the

A wash of clear water can be applied over applied pastel, with a watercolour brush, and the pastel can then be moved around, giving the effect of a watercolour. Pastel can be used on damp watercolour paper to pick out detail or emphasize a point. If you use this technique, always give the drawing a good spray of fixative when you finish, because the water breaks down the binder in the pastel and you need to add a bit of strength to it with fixative.

blended areas will appear deeper in tone and more solid because the colour is forced into the depressions in the paper.

It is best to work quickly at the beginning of a drawing to get down the essentials of the composition, and to slow up as the work progresses and draws to a conclusion in order to spend a lot of time considering, reflecting on and refining its balance, structure and meaning.

Pastel painting differs from pastel drawing or sketching in that in painting several layers of pastel are built up, and there are many techniques you can use. The subject of your work, the amount of time you have to work on it and what you feel and wish to express about it, will all dictate your approach. You will find that certain subjects need a loose drawing or sketching approach and others a more complete study – pastel painting.

THE BASICS

Pastels provide a very quick and direct way of working. They come in various forms – as pencils, hard and soft pastels – and it is worth trying them all, as each is best suited to particular techniques. Colour, tone and composition are all important aspects of pastel painting and drawing, and an understanding of them will strengthen your work. One of the joys of using pastels is the many ways in which they can be applied and the wonderful colour effects that can be achieved through these techniques.

Pastels can be blended smooth or applied and left as distinct marks or solid areas of colour.

Materials

The effects and techniques that are possible with pastels are increasing as more and more contemporary artists take up this versatile medium.

One should think of pastel painting as a union of two elements, the pastel and the paper, and it is important to have an understanding of these materials. To talk of 'the' pastel is in a way inaccurate, for several good types of pastel are available.

Pastel is made from artist-quality pigment, the same pigment that is used to make watercolour, gouache and oil paints. The difference between these materials lies in the binding medium that holds the pigment together. Pastel is made very simply; the dry pigment is mixed with a very weak solution of gum tragacite and water. The sticks are then rolled out or pressed into shape. The proportion of gum to water holds the key to the type of pastel you will be working with. Each one has a different quality and should be selected to suit the work you propose doing.

A bit of advance planning is very important – always try out the pastels and paper you are intending to use before committing yourself. A few tiny doodles with different colours and papers can be a revelation, and ten minutes of experimentation can save you hours of exasperation.

Pastels are available as pastel pencils, hard pastels and soft pastels, and they are described separately in order to clarify their individual characteristics. This does not mean, however, that you should use any one type exclusively. In fact, the opposite is true. Soft pastels are frequently used over harder ones to give emphasis or to create a layered effect; a line made with a pastel pencil can be used to define detail on a soft-pastel drawing. This combining of different types of pastel is part of the pleasure of using this unique medium.

PASTEL PENCILS
Pastel pencils are suitable for fine work and can also be used successfully for crosshatching and subtle modelling. The pastel core of the pencil is exceptionally fragile so care should be taken not to drop them. Use a craft knife to sharpen the pencils since a conventional sharpener puts too much pressure on the core, causing it to snap. Once you have exposed the pastel core with the craft knife, rub it with a bit of sand or glass paper to make a fine point. Small blocks of sandpaper are sold for this purpose in artists' materials shops. You can, if you wish, sharpen the point to a wedge shape. With this point you can draw both thick and fine lines simply by rotating the pencil as you work.

The choice of support is important with pencils; a very smooth paper will not hold the line and a heavy texture breaks up the line. Cartridge paper or pastel boards work well. Tinted papers are also quite interesting to work on with pencils, and the tint helps to hold the composition together. As with everything in painting, the subject must dictate the approach.

HARD PASTELS
Hard pastels (sometimes also known as 'nu' pastels) are manufactured under several different brand names. The most commonly available are Conté crayons (see page 120); the colours are brilliant, and the texture is smooth and even. The greater amount of gum in the binding solution of hard pastels makes them stronger and harder than the soft pastels – an advantage if you want to have a pastel that you can use on the point for line as well as on the side for broad strokes. They make ideal companions for outdoor work – durable, able to survive a few knocks but soft enough for a sketch. A quick way of making a point is to snap the stick and use the sharp ends.

The choice of paper is important because hard pastels tend to flatten the surface of the paper as you work more than soft ones. You will find the paper compacting and the stick sliding over the surface if you work over an area too much. Once the paper's texture is flattened it cannot hold additional pastel, although you can spray the paper with a liberal amount of fixative as a last resort to give the paper a bit of tooth again if this starts to happen. This will enable you to add a few more strokes, but it is of limited assistance. It is far better to choose a paper with a strong surface – one of the pastel papers or, better still, a pastel board or an abrasive paper.

Hard pastels can be used as a drawing medium with watercolours; they are hard enough to stay together well on damp paper. You could also try using a light wash of plain water with hard pastel. The water will make the pastel act like a dense watercolour, and you

Thistles are a marvellous subject for pastel pencils as the feathery lines can only be made with well-sharpened points. An abrasive paper was used for this drawing in order to capture the deep colour of the flower. With a pastel paper it would have been difficult to get sufficient depth of colour from the pencils. Allow plenty of time for such a drawing; you must proceed with some caution since the lines cannot be erased on abrasive paper. The blended effect on the leaves was obtained by using a great deal of pastel line and then very gradually rubbing the lines together with the side of a finger. A spare piece of the paper was used to give the pencil point a very sharp edge.

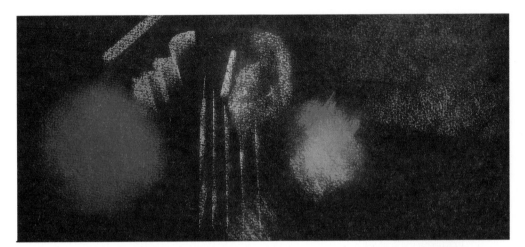

Left, hard pastels and below, soft pastels used on their sides and on the ends to create different types of marks. Varying pressures on the sticks have created different intensities of colour. Hard pastels have a crispness that is particularly attractive on dark papers.

will be able to work over certain areas with line or the side of the pastel when the paper dries.

SOFT PASTELS

Soft pastels are made with a small amount of gum binder. As a result, the sticks are soft enough to respond to the most subtle changes in pressure, giving an immediacy and sensitivity not matched by the harder pastels or any other media.

Used on their side, they enable you to cover large areas of the paper quickly, and a variety of colours can be laid over each other. If these layers are put on with a light touch, the colours underneath will be visible, forming a rich texture with some areas slightly picking up and blending with colours underneath. Layers can also be sprayed with fixative to keep the colours from mixing with one another if desired.

Soft pastel allows you to work from the lightest haze of colour to the densest mark with just a slight change of pressure on the stick. Yet even among the brands of soft pastels there are varying degrees of 'softness'.

The German pastels, Schmincke, and the French, Sennelier, are the softest obtainable. They are both very smooth and are made with fine pigment. They are quite delicate and should be treated with care. Rembrandt pastels also have fine colour, but are slightly harder than the others, which can be an advantage in some circumstances. (See page 120 for suppliers). Because of the low amount of gum in the binding solution of soft pastels, the sticks are very crumbly. It is best to keep them flat in a box or set. If they are loose, they make their own dust by rubbing

together and very soon you will have difficulty telling one colour from another.

If you want to clean pastels that have become covered in dust, put them in a plastic bag with some uncooked rice and shake the bag for a few moments. The rice will rub the surface dust off the pastel sticks, leaving them clean again.

A hard pastel in a dark colour was used on its end to draw in the outlines of the fruit. Hard pastels were used on their sides to put in tones and colours. The background was added by gently 'floating' over the surface of the paper with the flat side of the pastels. To do this, grip the pastel and pull it sideways, making sure your fingers don't touch the paper.

PRACTICE

Layer three colours one over another, and blend part of each layer. Continue the exercise, building up several different colours in layers. Try to end up with a variety of textures between blended and unblended areas.

LARGE SOFT PASTELS

Many students and professionals make their own pastels. These hand-made pastels are a bit cruder and heavier than the commercially manufactured ones, but they also have distinct advantages. They can be used to cover large areas quickly, and they have a resistance to crumbling when used on either a dry or a damp surface – both qualities that are important to the professional artist.

The colour manufacturers have been quick to respond to this development. Unison pastels (see page 120) include both brilliant colours and subtle, misty tones. Sennelier are now producing a range of short, large pastels and giant-sized pastels that are softer than Unison's.

Pastels can be used on bright-coloured paper for a bold effect.

Right, the peony was drawn with soft pastel on grey pastel board. The stem was drawn first, starting at the end and following the movement and line up to the head of the flower. The design of the white petals was put in with the side of the pastel, using marks to show the roundness of the form and also to create interesting abstract shapes. Alizarin crimson was put on small areas, some of which were spread and blended with a finger to make the pale pink tint of the petals. The leaves were drawn with a dark green, which was very gently overlaid with a light greyish-green.

SUPPORTS

The term support is used to describe any surface on which pastel can be used. Pastel is generally used on paper, but canvas or other materials can also serve to support the pastel. However, you cannot use pastel on an oil-based painting or an absolutely smooth surface.

Most of the pigment used in the manufacture of artists'-quality pastel is permanent or light-resistant; that is, it has the same or better life expectancy than most paints. However, the support or paper used can create problems when it comes to permanency. A paper with a large component of wood pulp, or any paper that is not acid-free, will eventually turn brown and this will obviously affect the work.

Wood-pulp paper, which includes newsprint, sugar paper and cardboard, will disintegrate without careful conservation. Frequently painters have used cardboard – Toulouse-Lautrec, for instance – and museums spend large sums of money and many hours of restoration trying to keep the work stabilized in good condition.

This does not mean that inexpensive papers should never be used. There is a time and place for them. It is liberating and immensely important to feel free to work and take chances, and experimentation with inexpensive materials allows you to do this. Nothing stunts the development of a student – or professional – as much as a feeling that 'This is it! This drawing has

anxiety. The more worry, the worse it will go.

If the drawing can't be drawn over to make a correction, you may have to erase it. Then your first concern should be to avoid damaging the surface or texture of the paper you are working on. A heavy scrubbing with a conventional eraser will flatten the texture so that subsequent layers of pastels will not hold or stick properly. You will find the pastel sliding over the paper instead of biting into it. Fresh bread is the most desirable and professional way to erase pastel, Conté or charcoal. This may seem strange, but the moisture in the bread lifts the pastel off, without damaging the paper. Even the deepest colours can be taken off. If a slight image remains, this can be worked on with a kneaded or putty eraser. Bear in mind, though, that the light lines or ghost images where, for instance, Degas moved an arm or redefined a form were part of the charm and interest in the drawing and not a blemish!

With some pastel papers, it is advisable to scratch off the mark lightly with a blade. If you are working on abrasive paper, the only thing for it is to press a bit of masking tape over the offending area and gently pull it off with the pastel hoping not to remove part of the paper surface at the same time.

GOOD-QUALITY PASTEL PAPERS
Selection of the right type of paper for the subject is as important as the right pastel. There are three questions you should ask yourself when choosing a paper: Do I want to do a quick sketch or a pastel painting that will require layering? Do I want a tinted or coloured background to bring out the tones of a pale subject or a light paper to contrast with a darker subject? Do I want the background the paper will give me to be a warm or cool colour? Once you have answered these questions you will have narrowed down your options enough to make a good choice.

For a simple drawing, one of the lightweight Fabriano or Hanemuhle Ingres papers would do. They are very lightfast and come in a variety of tints and colours. Less expensive cartridge paper can be used, but has the minimum acceptable amount of tooth. A better choice in this price range is Bockingford.

If you want to do a pastel painting that will require

to be terrific!' All artists make mistakes; they would not make any real breakthroughs if they did not. When a painting is a 'total disaster', you feel free to do outrageous things with it, and these are like the alchemist's lead that turns to pure gold.

Pastel is a very forgiving medium. It is easily erased or drawn over. However, the best advice is to keep drawing and not stop to make erasures because rhythm of work is important for good observation. Nothing is as corrosive to drawing or painting as layering, a paper with a strong texture is called for – this, listed in order of gripping power can be water-colour paper, a pastel board, or abrasive paper. A fine-quality, heavier paper, acid free and 40 per cent cotton for durability, is Fabriano's Tiziano. It has a good surface suitable for pastel paintings, and is available in 30 colours and black. (See page 120 for a list of distributors of pastel papers and boards.)

There are new ranges of pastel boards on the market. These give you a slightly abrasive, velvet surface that holds the pastel well but still allows smooth blending. And the work does not have to be sprayed. There is one drawback with this excellent support – the textured surface has a water-based binding solution holding it to the board. All dampness must be avoided, including contact with damp fingers, or the surface will lift off.

ABRASIVE PAPERS

Not many people realize that they can buy pastel paper at the ironmongers (hardware store). The finest grade of sand or glass paper, 00 (flour paper), makes an unusual surface to work on. Some people call it the pastel-maker's delight because it consumes so much of the pastel. Nonetheless, the effect is quite stunning, resembling a fresh oil painting, but with the clarity and matt surface of pastel.

The paper manufacturers have now brought out their own abrasive pastel papers. These have a finer surface than sandpaper, they are available in either grey or beige tints, and come in large sheets. The amount of pastel that would be used on a full-sized sheet is too much to bear thinking about, and for economy's sake it is better to use small squares of sandpaper, or cut up the artists'-quality sheets into smaller pieces. You cannot blend on this type of paper, but you can over-draw because the paper can hold all that lovely colour so well.

TINTED AND COLOURED PASTEL PAPERS

Originally pastel was used on either plain or grey-blue paper, but now a great variety of possibilities are available. There are very subtle tints that are useful for all subjects, and bright colours for a bolder effect. It is much easier to bring out a light subject if you use a tinted or dark-toned paper.

WATERCOLOUR PAPER

Watercolour paper is an ideal support for pastel paintings. It has enough strength to be worked over several times and the paper can be given a light wash of colour before you begin. Make sure you choose a paper with some tooth. A hot-pressed or smooth paper will not hold the pastel sufficiently.

BLENDING TOOLS

Nature has given us the best blending tools in our fingers and hands. Use a little finger for detail and the side of your hand to sweep across an area and blend it back. These are the driest parts of the hand, which is

Left, this drawing of a hybrid tea rose was done with soft pastel on Fabriano (artist's) abrasive paper. The serrated edge of the leaf was drawn with the point of the stick, then the colour was pulled inwards with a finger.

Right, this study of a bearded iris shows what can happen if you dare to use a very strong colour in the background. French ultramarine was used to complement the warm orange and pinks of the flower.

   Once the flower was drawn, the blue background was put in with the side of a soft pastel and blended smooth. The flower was then strengthened, and simplified by blending the colours and increasing the highlights, which stand out well against the dark tone of blue.

   The leaves were darkened so that they are not the same tone as the background. When you make a fundamental change in a work, the rest must be brought in line with the change.

what you need to blend without smudging. Torchons – sticks of rolled-up blotting paper – can be used for detail, but they tend to push off the pastel as they blend, whereas with a finger you can gently push it in.

THE FINISHED WORK

It is advisable to give a light fixative spray to a finished work. Although the fixative will push back some light tones, the effect with the modern sprays is quite minimal, if used sparingly. Even if a work is immediately framed behind glass the unfixed pastel dust will drift down slowly to settle on the mount board. When spraying, hold the can at least 1ft (30cm) away from the paper, moving it continuously. Many artists economize by using hair spray as a substitute for artists' fixative, but it is not to be recommended because the spray is harsh and uneven.

   Remember to spray only in a well-ventilated room and away from any open flame. If you are allergic to fixative, or for other health reasons such as pregnancy wish to avoid inhaling the fumes, you could try using a weak solution of gelatin and water. Use ½ teaspoon of gelatin to 2 pt/1 litre of water, and allow the mixture to stand for a couple of hours. Then dissolve it in a double-boiler, and apply it with a diffuser, which you can buy from an artists' materials shop.

Colour

Left, predominantly warm colours have been used, set off by the very cool violet shadow and blue-greens of the leaves.

Right, cool blues and greens and lemon yellow are set off by the warm beige in the background.

Pastels are actually solid sticks of paint. They can be used for drawing, of course, but they also have the greater dimension of paint to offer the artist.

There are special considerations to be taken into account when we discuss pastel colour. Artists'-quality pigment, chalk and a weak solution of gum and water are used to make the sticks. In this process, pure pigment is used to produce the basic colours. The pigment to lighten the tone and black to darken the tone of the original pure colour. For example, a pale pink is alizarin crimson stepped up in tone several wrappers, and these are created by adding white pigment to lighten the tone and black to darken the tone of the original pure colour. For example, a pale pink is alizarin crimson stepped up in tone several times. Each time, one half of the colour is mixed with the equivalent amount of white until the very lightest pink is obtained. A pale yellow may have one part cadmium yellow to five parts white.

The one besetting sin of pastels is their tendency to look chalky. This happens when the artist uses too many colours that contain a high proportion of white, which impairs the chromatic (colour) value of the work. This need never happen if you keep the problem in mind, and avoid using too many of the light tones together. Even a slight amount of clear colour will quickly restore the balance if the painting starts to look chalky. Each medium has its problems; oil paints become muddy if not handled properly, watercolours appear lifeless if too much water is used, and pastel looks chalky if you use only the palest tints.

SELECTING YOUR COLOURS
It is not necessary to have a huge box of pastels to begin with, but you will need the basic colours and at least a few tones of each of these colours. You can buy

a box of pre-selected colours, or build up your own selection by buying them individually. If you are going to specialize in a particular subject, such as landscape or portraiture, you can get boxed sets of the colours you will be most likely to need, but if you buy boxed sets, you will need to add additional light and dark tones of the colours included.

If you want to buy individual pastels, avoid confusion in the early stages by starting with the basics. The primary colours are red, yellow and blue. These colours cannot be created by mixing. They exist as they are in nature, which is why they are called the primaries. All the other colours can, in theory, be mixed from them.

A basic range of colours should include: ivory, yellow, yellow ochre, red, rose, sienna, blue, light green (one that has some yellow in it), emerald green (turquoise), dark blue, burnt umber and black.

Artists are always referring to warm or cool colours. An easy way to remember this is to refer to colours as the colours of fire and the colours of cool water.

THE WARM PALETTE

The warm colours, listed and graded by intensity, are: cadmium orange, red, cadmium yellow, yellow ochre and burnt sienna, lemon yellow (which contains a cool green tint), and rose/alizarin crimson (which contains a blue tint).

THE COOL PALETTE

The cool colours, listed and graded by intensity, are: emerald green/viridian, permanent green, cobalt blue, ultramarine blue and prussian blue, French ultramarine (which contains crimson), indigo (a natural dye from the indigo plant, it has a warm tint) and violet (which contains red).

The complementary contrast of the red flowers against the green paper makes the flowers glow with light. Violet and blue-green add interest in the shadow areas.

HOW COLOURS WORK

Warm colours appear to come forward since they are brighter and hotter than the cool colours. This is important to remember when you are working on a landscape, or even a still life.

The colours leading the warm and cool lists are the extremes, and as such clash or are discordant when they are close together. This is not to imply that these colours should never be used together. Discord, as well as harmony, are useful modes of expression in art. The painter Vlaminck used orange and viridian together to produce vibrant landscapes. Edvard Munch also used colour clashes to express emotions.

THE COMPLEMENTARY COLOURS

Certain pairs of colours work very well together, making each other look more vibrant and beautiful, and they are known as complementary colours: red and green, yellow and purple, and orange and blue. A good composition usually makes use of one of these complementary pairs. This doesn't mean that a red and green composition doesn't have other colours in it, just that the combination of red and green in that work predominates over the other colours.

If you put two pieces of paper with complementary colours of the same tone close together, for example a red and green, they will appear to shimmer. This is

Persimmons on yellow paper. Two complementary pairs – yellow and mauve and red and green – were used for a very bright and lively effect.

Orange and blue are complementary colours and used together make each other sing. The orange, being warmer, advances against the blue.

caused by the eye jumping from one to the other. The movement of the eye is so rapid that you are unaware of it. If you remove the cards you will still see the ghosts of the red and green shapes but their positions will now be reversed, the red appearing where the green was and a slight green ghost where the red was, such is the power of the complementary colours to dazzle the eye.

This dazzle is also the reason why shadows may take on the hue of the complementary colour of an object. The Impressionists noted that wheat and hay in strong sunlight appeared to have violet shadows, while red poppies had cool green tones in their shadows. The Impressionists made use of the phenomenon of complementary colours to create landscape paintings that have an atmosphere of eternal light.

PRACTICE

Look at a book of Matisse's or Picasso's work and try to pick out the different complementary sets of colours that they have used in different paintings.

Draw a red apple and then add its shadow on the table in yellow-green.

Step 1 *Far left, the dawn was just breaking on a clear day, but the hillside seemed to be still slumbering under a soft blue mantle, providing an opportunity for an experiment with very strong, Fauvist colour. The hillside was drawn with French ultramarine blue and its complementary colour, orange. The soft pastel was allowed to run very freely over the surface.*

Step 2 *Left, the drawing was done very quickly. By the time the trees had been added in the foreground, the sun had risen and the blue shadows had disappeared, taking the magical light with them.*

Tonal Values and Colour

Step 1 *Four strongly contrasting tones were chosen for this drawing of a monastery on the Greek island of Corfu in order to give an impression of the clear, white light of Greece. The tones were tried out on the paper first.*

First the shapes were loosely blocked in, and the dark tones were stepped down in a diagonal line to the base of the monastery. This will focus the eye on the building as the centre of interest in the composition. One important use of tone is to create the centre of interest.

Step 2 *A great change in the composition occurred with the addition of the background tones. These were left out of the first stage of the drawing to show how important it is to have a strong contrast behind the white monastery. The composition now looks whole.*

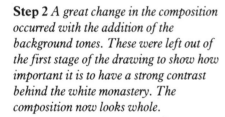

There is frequent confusion about what is meant by tone, as opposed to colour. To put it simply, tone is the amount of darkness or lightness of any colour. Pink is a light tone of red, ivory is a light tone of yellow ochre; navy blue and pale blue are different tones of the same colour.

A strong tonal structure is absolutely vital in a composition and you need to understand how to create this before plunging into full colour. There is no reason, of course, why tonal compositions have to be dull or unattractive. Pure black, white and grey can be a bit grim, but there is no reason to use this limited range. Try instead a mixture of warm greys, which have just a slight amount of brown in them, and cool greys – good mixers with indigo blue, as you would expect. This gives you a much wider selection and the potential for a more interesting composition.

Step 3 *Right, some of the tones in the foreground were lightly blended to bring it together, and a few shadows were added on the side of the monastery. A tonal composition that includes warmer tones rather than just black, white and grey, can have an elegance that many colourful paintings lack.*

Left, a tonal drawing of an old umbrella pine, made using different shades of grey pastel.

Below, the same structure of tones was used in the full colour study. If you make a tonal sketch prior to a full colour study, use that sketch as a guide to the values of the colours you should use. Try to match the light and dark of the colours you use to the tones in the tonal sketch.

This shows how, with four tones, you can simplify a subject and create a feeling of space. The tones have been alternated back through the scene in clearly delineated bands, with the lightest and darkest tones next to each other in the nearer part of the picture, and the mid tones in the distance.

Paradoxically, the way to fabulous colour is through limited colour. Different colours cannot all sing on the same note – some must take precedence. A lemon yellow beside a light blue looks dreadful, but change the blue to the deepest tone of navy and you have a stunning effect. Complementary colours will be more effective if they are not both the same tone in a composition.

In a class, students sometimes ask what colour they should make the background or object in their composition, and the best response is: do you want it to be light or dark? Before you decide on the colour to use, consider the tone of the colour.

The importance of tone is based on the fact that our eyes perceive and 'read' brightness and darkness before they read colour. We also dream in black and white – colour rarely enters into a dream. The mind, obviously content with tone, presents a 'shorthand' of the whole reality.

This is also apparent in the way black and white films and photographs were quickly accepted when they were first used. Colour is glorious, but colour that is not based on a good tonal structure can be insipid and confusing.

DO'S AND DON'TS

Do experiment with different coloured papers.

Do try to keep on drawing over any mistakes you have made rather than erasing them because rhythm of work is important for good observation.

Do make some trial sketches to check the tonal structure of a drawing before you begin.

Do try different tones of the complementary colours together.

Do experiment with compositions in a range of warm and cool greys.

Don't use too many light tones together as this will make the picture look chalky.

A grey tone was used to draw a quick note of a grape vine. This shows how effective even one tone can be in defining a form. The diagonal cast shadow gives an indication of space and roots the vine to the ground.

A tonal study of trees. It was quite late in the afternoon, and the trees had the light behind them, creating elegant shapes. The sketch was done in a few minutes, using three tones.

A small sketchbook drawing made while looking down on a Romanesque chapel. In this landscape there were a great many different shades of green, which have been condensed into a few tones. There was little time to do the drawing, and a tonal sketch was a more effective way to define the shapes than a conventional drawing done in the same limited time.

TONAL STRUCTURE

If you were to look at a painting in which the tones of all the colours were the same, you would have more difficulty in understanding that painting than one that was done in tones of white, black and grey. The tones give the work its structure, or bones.

When you plan a work, think about the composition in terms of tones first. This is important with pastels, because you may be deciding on a tinted background or coloured paper for the subject. First decide whether the object you are interested in drawing or painting is a light, medium or dark tone. If it is a bouquet of daffodils, a medium or dark tone of paper will bring out the pale colour. Conversely, a dark subject can be put on a medium tone, or, for increased intensity, on a pale colour. Make a few small trial sketches on the tail end of the paper before beginning, to see how strong

the contrast will be between the paper and the main subject of the work.

Once you have made your decision on the background, look for the lights and darks in your subject. In pastel, the darks are generally put in first. The more you are able to keep the colours in distinct grades of tone, the stronger and more effective the painting will be. There should be strong darks, medium tones and clear, light tones. If most of the colours are medium tones, the work will lack definition and energy. There is a very easy way to check the tonal structure of a work. Turn it upside down and look at it from across the room. You will now be looking at the abstract design of the composition rather than the drawing. Any deficiencies in the structure will be more obvious to you, and easy to correct.

Composition

Composition is a rather grand term for the
organization of the elements in a painting. Many
people think that there is some complicated,
intellectual theory governing composition in fine art,
but in fact you probably already know a lot more about
it than you realize.

Arranging a composition is not that different from
deciding on clothes, decor or gardens, so why don't we
use our sense of style or rightness when it comes to
painting? A basic rule is to follow your own taste and
sense of appropriateness.

There are rules of composition and they are
probably familiar to you under a different guise.

A work should have a centre of interest. That is, one
part of the work should dominate and be the *raison
d'etre* for the painting. The other parts should support
this area, not overwhelm it or distract from it.

Left, the jagged edges of the hills are the important factor in this sketch. The sharp contrast of tones and crosshatching emphasize the lines and angles that were apparent from this high viewpoint. A good approach to composition is to draw lines to mark out the shapes and then to compose the drawing inside this frame.

Below, although trees are usually thought of as being upright, these woods have been drawn without a single vertical line. The whole composition is based on curves and diagonals. The curves echo the harmony and graceful gesture of the trees, the diagonal lines help the feeling of soft, bending wood. The diagonal is also a more dynamic line in a composition than a vertical line.

With this subject it was difficult to avoid a symmetrical composition. All the angles apparent in the scene were used to contrast with the great arch of the old stone bridge. Crosshatching is by far the quickest way to make a note of tone and angle. Remember to lighten the crosshatching to create a sense of distance and space.

The centre of interest should not be placed directly in the middle of the picture. Symmetrical compositions are not as interesting to the eye as asymmetrical arrangements. It is better to have a little diversity of shape and arrangement on the paper. Just think what it would be like if a musician played the same note over and over again. You can, of course, push diversity too far; then you have disharmony.

COMPOSING A STILL LIFE
The selection of props will be vital to the success of the work. This doesn't mean they have to be expensive or elaborate. Simple items from around the house or kitchen make very interesting combinations. You should look, above all, for a diversity of shapes.

One item should be larger than all the rest. There should be at least two smaller objects, not the same

Above, a quick sketch exploring the problem of suggesting a great distant plain beyond the rocks in the foreground. Warm yellow and mauve were used for the rocks in the foreground and a pale blue for the distant landscape. The shapes interlock to create an interesting composition.

Right, to create the sense of the hills almost disappearing into the distance, the tones were graded lighter and lighter towards the back of the drawing, which gives an illusion of depth.

Above, the trees stretched along the road in a great arc receding into the distance. To get that feeling of space, the trees were drawn diminishing in size as they go back, and also less distinctively. Objects close up are usually drawn with a heavier and sharper line to bring them into focus.

The striking feature here was the enormous contrast in scale between the man-made objects of house and orchard and the enormity and strength of the natural form of the cliff face. The house and trees have been placed in the lower half of the picture area to exaggerate the sense of the cliff looming over them.

Step 1 *The rough stone texture of the house contrasted with the diagonal branches and the soft foliage. Two different greens were used for the large areas of foliage in front of and behind the house to separate them and give a sense of space.*

Step 2 *Warm colours and the young tree were added in the foreground, and the viewpoint was slightly altered so that the curve of the tree was set off against the angle of the house. No blending has been done yet.*

size, and one or more objects smaller still. Be aware of the importance of texture, in particular, when you are working with pastels – for example, a rough piece of pottery combined with something smooth, such as fruit and a basket, or glass and dried flowers. Even a mundane group of items such as an old coal shovel, a piece of wood and a polished copper coal scuttle can provide a challenging subject.

Step 3 *Right, in the final stage certain areas have been blended back to set a deeper and smoother tone of one colour against the rough texture of another; for example, the smooth areas of foliage against the textured surface of the house. This part of the work should never be rushed.*

APPROACHES TO COMPOSITION
At the beginning of the 20th century, artists began to break away from classical composition and experimented with what is now called romantic composition. In classical composition the artist drew or painted images within the contained world of the

picture frame. The frame formed a boundary around a balanced, harmonious and inward-looking composition. In the new age of composition, however, images became clips from a larger composition – life.

Edgar Degas was one of the leaders of this new development, with his fondness for experimentation. He frequently used cropped compositions for his racecourse paintings, in which part of a horse might be out of the picture frame. In a portrait, a bowl of

flowers might dominate, with the sitter almost off the canvas. He used this new approach to composition to create excitement, tension and intimacy in his work. Looking at his pictures, the viewer has the feeling of being at the race-course or in a room with the washerwoman. He pushed out against the confining rigour of classical composition, to the edge of disharmony, but since he was a master he never fell into chaos.

Theories and mathematics have their place, but to see the effect of good composition in practice there is no better place to look than in an artist's sketchbook. The notes an artist makes say a lot about the way he or she works, and what they are looking for. A strong composition is very important in painting, so when you take notes, think about the potential for making an interesting and dynamic arrangement of shapes.

This was the preparatory sketch for the drawing on page 75. It is easier to understand the structure of the larger work by looking at the sketch. The horizon and tower were deliberately placed off-centre, and the marks of the outline framework are still visible. The clouds were drawn as a sweeping curve against the upright form of the chapel.

DO'S AND DON'TS

Do give your work a centre of interest, and don't allow other areas to detract from it.

Do make sure a drawing has a diversity of shapes and that the shapes vary in size.

Don't place your centre of interest directly in the middle of the picture.

The heather and broom were on a bank above eye level, and were placed high in the picture. A few lines were used to indicate the position of the major shapes – if this sketch doesn't work as an interesting pattern or design, the final painting will not work as well. The drawing was then developed in terms of colour and texture.

Left, the stone face of this house, perched on the side of a hill, caught the last rays of the sun; the rest of the house was shaded by the chestnut wood. The sharp diagonal lines of the hill, the house and the branches above the roof made a strong composition.

PRACTICE

Cut out a rectangular shape in a piece of card. Looking through this card, 'frame' a composition of a landscape or still life and then make a drawing kit.

When you have finished your drawing, move closer to the centre of interest and frame and sketch a detail of the original composition.

Techniques

The pear was drawn using just two shades of green with the pastel sticks held on their sides, and the marks have been left unblended. This is the simplest way of using pastel.

Step 1 *Rough marks of soft pastel were used to define the shape of the vase.*

In this drawing of a nectarine, soft pastels were used and the colours were blended with a little finger to create a soft, smooth effect.

Step 2 *The colour was developed and a cool blue was added for the table top.*

The pastel stick is supremely responsive to the slightest change in pressure. To achieve all of the possible variations of tone and colour it is important to learn how to manipulate the stick freely. Soft pastel is not used like a pencil or crayon; generally the stick is held at an acute angle to the paper, with the point and part of the side in contact with the paper at the same time. This allows you to change the width and shape of the mark as you draw. It is important not to clutch the pastel tightly as you would a pencil.

For large areas use the pastel on its side varying the pressure to create solid or lighter areas of colour. When using pastel on its side make sure your fingers don't touch the paper as they will drag a line across it. The points or edges of hard pastel are good for line drawing and cross-hatching.

Step 3 *Rich colours were layered and scumbled over the vase to pull it together.*

Step 4 *Lemon yellow and a warm ochre were drawn over the blue in the background to give the effect of warm light coming through a window, which gives harmony to the drawing.*

'MIXING' PASTEL COLOUR

The basic difference between pastel and paints is obvious. Instead of mixing colours on a palette until you have what you want, you select pre-mixed colours and apply them directly to the paper, using various techniques to adjust colours and tones on the paper. An ingenious number of attractive techniques have been developed for this purpose. Of course, in your box you may find exactly the right colour, which you can use on its own. However, the mixing techniques are part of the unique charm of pastels, even when they are not absolutely necessary in order to gain a particular colour.

There are two basic methods of mixing pastel. The

Soft pastels were used on their sides to show what can be accomplished without blending or extensive drawing. With controlled light pressure on the pastel it was possible to define the flower clearly.

Right, the paper was first given a light rubbing over with charcoal, and the drawing was then done with pastels. The two have blended together to create a range of rich, dark colours and tones.

first and simplest is direct blending – that is, blending them with your finger, a tissue or a torchon. The second is visual blending, when colours are applied in such a way that they mix in the eye of the person looking at the painting.

DIRECT BLENDING

To blend directly, apply the colour with the side of the pastel. Use the point for very small areas only. Once this first layer of pastel is in place, a second or third colour can be laid lightly over it. These layers can then be blended together using either a little finger or the side of a hand, or a torchon for small details (see page 20/21).

VISUAL BLENDING

All of the following techniques have in common the fact that the colours are blended by the eye of the person looking at them, instead of on the paper by the artist. Visual blending depends on creating broken colour, that is, lots of little specks of colour that merge together in the eye of the viewer. These techniques include scumbling, feathering, cross-hatching and pointillism.

SCUMBLING WITH SOFT PASTELS

With scumbling, the pastel colours are layered loosely, one on top of the other. Sometimes the first layer is

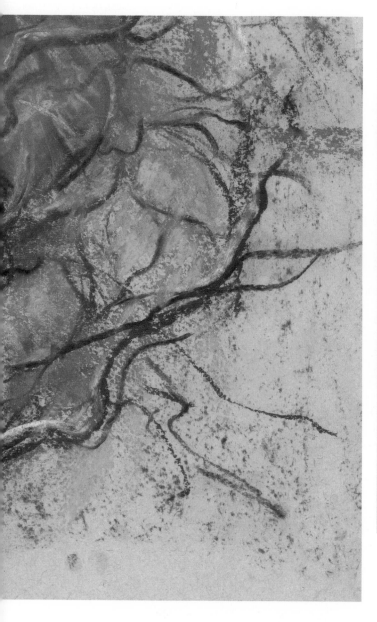

Feathering was used to build up a rich, complex, woven effect of colours that merge together into light and shadow areas on the pot.

put in more or less evenly, and the second layer is applied with the side of a soft pastel in a small circular or scribble pattern. It is best to use a small piece of pastel for this work. The layers form an intricate loose pattern of colour similar to a tapestry. Many layers can be applied in this manner to build up the overall effect.

There is no direct blending as the object of this technique is to look through the layers of colours, allowing the eye to blend them.

Although a slight mixing of the layers as they are added is desirable, you can spray each layer with fixative to keep the colours separate.

PASTEL AND CHARCOAL

One technique that is particularly effective is that of working pastel into a base layer of soft charcoal. To do this, rub a light watercolour paper with a block of scene-painters' charcoal. Then draw into it with pastel. The pastel colours turn into a variety of subtle shades when they mix with the loose charcoal. If too much charcoal is used the effect will be muddy. It is best to err on the side of caution and use very little to begin with.

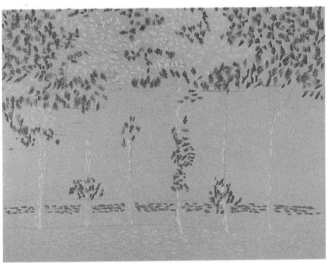

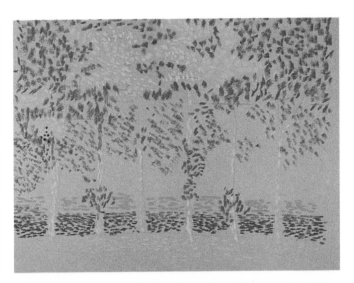

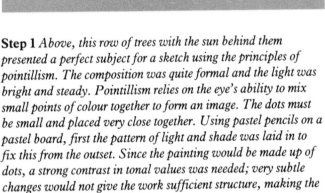

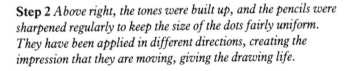

Step 1 *Above, this row of trees with the sun behind them presented a perfect subject for a sketch using the principles of pointillism. The composition was quite formal and the light was bright and steady. Pointillism relies on the eye's ability to mix small points of colour together to form an image. The dots must be small and placed very close together. Using pastel pencils on a pastel board, first the pattern of light and shade was laid in to fix this from the outset. Since the painting would be made up of dots, a strong contrast in tonal values was needed; very subtle changes would not give the work sufficient structure, making the composition weak and feeble.*

Step 2 *Above right, the tones were built up, and the pencils were sharpened regularly to keep the size of the dots fairly uniform. They have been applied in different directions, creating the impression that they are moving, giving the drawing life.*

Step 3 *Right, shadows were added to the upper part of the tree trunks to darken them, which increases the impression of dense foliage casting a heavy shadow over the tree. Cast shadows from the trees were also added, which improved the composition by giving structure and weight to the base of the painting.*

Step 4 *Previous page, to finish, the river bank on the far side was just barely indicated with light tones. One of the pleasures with this type of drawing is the ability to come back to it and add a bit more work from time to time, slowly building it up in layers and improving it. It is interesting to see just how far you can take a drawing in this way.*

PRACTICE

Fill a page with as many types of marks as possible, and vary the pressure on the pastel from the lightest touch to full strength. Turn the pastel stick as you make a mark, use the side, or whatever you can think of to get to know the possibilities of the pastel marks before you begin drawing with it. Try arranging the marks in an abstract pattern, blending some areas with a finger, scumbling over others. You can intensify or tone down a colour by feathering over it.

FEATHERING WITH HARD PASTELS OR PASTEL PENCILS

Feathering is generally used with hard pastels, as the pastel can be sharpened to a fine point. Short, thin, parallel lines are drawn close together with the point of the pastel. The fine feather pattern can be used to build up a complete work or to soften hard edges by drawing over them.

An area that is too heavy or bright can easily be modified, or 'pushed back', with a light or dark tone feathered over it. A cool tint can be added over a warm colour to cool it down, and a warm colour can be added over a cool one to warm it up.

CROSSHATCHING WITH HARD PASTEL OR PASTEL PENCILS

Crosshatching is a traditional technique in charcoal and pencil drawing. With pastel, you have the possibilities provided by the added dimension of colour. The principle is the same in black and white or colour: lines are drawn parallel to each other, and another set of lines, which can be a different colour, are added over them in another direction so that they 'cross' the first lines. Closely drawn lines produce quite a strong tone that can be used to model the form or to put in shadows.

POINTILLISM

Pointillism was developed by Georges Seurat in the 1880s. It can be described as an extreme form of Impressionism, where the light that illuminates the forms is expressed as hundreds of small dots – tiny points of clear colour – that are visually mixed by the eye, coalescing into a solid form. The colour theory behind true pointillism is very complicated, but we can experiment with a simplified version of it. Modern colour printing is also based on the use of tiny dots that our eyes read as solid areas of colours. The smaller the dots, the more even the blend.

Pointillism is a very interesting and informative technique to use throughout a work, not just to modify certain areas. It demands a great deal of time and patience, of course. Hard pastels are best for pointillism because they can be sharpened. Use them on a small piece of abrasive paper or coloured paper for the best effect.

Using the pointillist technique again, just the dark tones around the base and top of the pear were put in to begin with, and these defined its shape. Medium and light tones were added to the pear to create the shadow. Highlights were added to the right-hand side of the pear to separate that edge from the background.

DO'S AND DON'TS

Do use the pastel on its side for large areas and on the point for drawing and details.

Do use hard pastels for feathering as they can be sharpened to a point.

Do keep the dots small when using a pointillist technique.

Don't clutch the pastel tightly as you draw, but keep your hand and arm relaxed.

Frottage

The method known as frottage is a good introduction to using pastels. Frottage isn't a new technique at all; artists have used it for centuries. It consists of placing a piece of paper on a raised or textured surface – a flat rock, bark, or a rough wall – and rubbing over it with a stick of pastel. As the stick is rubbed over the paper, it picks up the image underneath, creating an interesting textured surface. One of the best-known examples of frottage is brass rubbing.

This technique does not rely heavily on drawing skills and is a good way to get going with the medium and lose one's inhibitions about using the pastel sticks. Pastel is not a medium for tentative, light drawings. The more pastel that goes on the paper, the better the drawing usually turns out. Pastel is not used like an oil crayon, for line or filling in shapes. You paint with it; putting layer upon layer, rubbing the colour back with your hand and redrawing on the blended areas, until you are building up the form in rather the same way that a sculptor uses clay. If, after three hours of drawing, you are well and truly covered with pastel, you will probably have done a good drawing and will have moved your work ahead.

Frottage can also be used with graphite or crayon, but pastel will give you several additional possibilities over the other mediums. You can use as many colours as you wish, and the colours will slightly mix or blend when you make more than one rubbing on a sheet. The amount of mixing can be controlled by spraying between layers with fixative. This is only the first stage, however.

The frottage can subsequently be worked on and developed into a full-scale drawing or painting by blending and drawing over the top of the rubbed image. The reason for using frottage in the first instance is to give yourself an interesting base of texture or pattern to work into. The blank page can be very intimidating, and a good texture and design on the paper gets you going. Even Van Gogh used to wipe his brushes over a new white canvas to break the intimidating white expanse.

The other advantage of using frottage is more subtle. Nature has a very complicated rhythm of shape and movement. Frequently the shapes of a cloud can be seen in the textures of a stone or a piece of dry wood. The waves of the sea can resemble the swirls

Step 3 *Right, the shapes of the trees were drawn in with an indication of the light. The drawing was lightly blended to push back the image and sprayed with fixative. The light tones on the trees and in the foliage were picked out, and a few details in the background were suggested with a light line.*

Step 1 *Pale green pastel paper was taped securely to a stone, and a very dark brown, soft pastel was rubbed gently over it to give the deep shaded effect of a wood.*

Step 2 *The paper was moved on to another stone, which had sharp lines gouged into the surface. A russet colour was rubbed over this to create a base for the forest floor.*

50

and knots of old trees. As natural forms are repeated in other elements we can use one as a basis for another.

There is no way we can draw the minute changes and subtlety of natural forms. They are far too complex and diverse. We can learn from them, however, which is another great use of frottage. The rubbing can be studied in detail to analyse the changes of scale in natural objects. The lines of movement can be seen frozen like a fossil in amber.

THE TECHNIQUE

Before you begin work, select the paper carefully. Avoid thick or heavy papers; they will not be pliable enough to fit into the depressions and pick up the detail of the surface you will be rubbing. You have to use fairly soft paper to pick up the texture underneath. However, if the paper is too thin – for example, rice

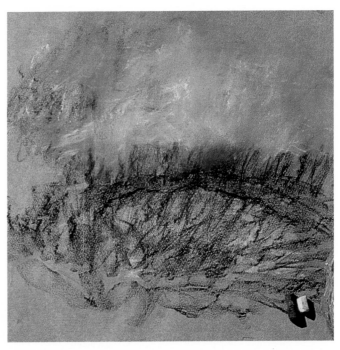

Step 1 *To capture the sunlight at the edge of the wood, three colours were used on warm grey paper taped to a flat stone. The paper was repositioned at a different angle for each colour.*

A dull alizarin-grey pastel paper was placed against a tree stump and rubbed with a dark grey pastel. The rubbing was slightly blended, and the stump was drawn over the texture and highlighted with pale green.

Step 2 *The frottage was given a spray of fixative to hold the colours and prevent them mixing too heavily with the drawing that would be added on top. The trees were drawn in with a dark brown pastel and highlighted with white.*

paper – it may tear when you rub over it with the pastel. A bit of experimentation is essential. Remember that you can also use tinted paper. Your selection of pastels is quite important, too. Generally one of the harder types of soft pastel is more suitable than the very soft ones, which fill up the paper too quickly and smother the design.

Since all paper surfaces are different, it would be wise to try out a few on the object before you begin. Place the paper you have selected on the textured or raised surface. Stones and wood are very suitable for rubbing, as are walls.

It is necessary to hold the paper firmly in place with some masking tape as you do the rubbing. Holding the pastel on its side and move it gently and evenly over the surface. You will have to use a half stick, or even a full stick of pastel, for this. A small piece will make a line rather than a flat, wide sweep of colour, which is what you need.

Step 3 *The drawing was finished in the studio. The softer, warm browns and the umbrella of leaves were added with soft pastels, while retaining the feeling of the light filtering through the dense canopy of leaves. The original frottage can be seen behind the drawing.*

Once you have your first rubbing you can begin drawing over it. However, you may wish to layer another rubbing onto it before starting the drawing. If the colour is very soft and mixes quickly, spray the first rubbing with fixative before taking subsequent rubbings. When you are satisfied with the textures and patterns you have obtained with the frottage, you can then start your drawing over the top, blending it or not as necessary.

The pleasure and value of frottage lies in the freedom and incentive it gives you to experiment with colour and texture and it eliminates the inhibiting effect of the blank paper.

THE
ELEMENTS

Pastels are suited to a variety of subjects. Their brilliant, luminous colours are wonderful for capturing the varied hues of flowers, whether soft and subtle or deep and rich. They are ideal for creating the textures of surfaces, whether hard and rough or smooth and glass-like. And landscapes and skies can be portrayed in all their variety, whether in a quick sketch on the spot or in a more studied painting in the studio.

The aim of this drawing was to express the feeling of space and movement and to give the viewer the feeling that they are looking up at a cloudscape. The point of light where the sun broke through is the important centre of interest in the composition. The sea was blended to give a strong contrast and base for the sky. The area under the cloud was kept very soft so that it would recede in the distance and give the illusion that the upper part of the cloud was moving forward.

Flowers

Each flower is an individual. The wisteria droops softly, grateful for the warmth of the sun. The rose seems aware of its beauty as it gracefully displays and unfolds. Each plant has developed its own personality and attractions to lure the bees and other pollinating insects. If you can capture some of the seductive quality of the bloom, the drawing will have greater life and an added dimension.

A flower should be observed as a whole together with its stems and leaves. Often a good drawing of a bloom is let down because too little time and care are given to the colour and shape of the leaves and the thickness of the stem.

Musicians and painters have a lot in common; they both try to express and give a form to emotions, places and concepts. A beautiful drawing and a figure are both based on firm disciplines and structures. In music, precisely measured time holds the piece together and gives it its form. In a drawing, visual measurement does this. The most inspired and passionate maestro quietly counts the beat as he

conducts the symphony orchestra. The modern painter runs his eye back and forth over the form, making mental notes of its height in relation to its width and depth. Where is the line of movement? Where does a curve oppose a straight line or angle? Henry Moore said that measurement is everything, the base even for abstract art. Flowers with their

This study of an iris was done on abrasive paper because the paper-thin petals needed only the barest touch of a soft pastel to capture their colour and delicacy. Since the abrasive paper 'grabs' the pastel it was possible to trip and glance lightly over the surface while drawing the lovely movement of the flower. Two colours, coral and turquoise, were layered very lightly in the background.

When wisteria first comes into bloom its leaves have lovely coppery tips. The drawing catches the softness of the blooms, while the strong viridian green in the background creates the excitement and energy characteristic of spring. This was drawn with large sticks of Unison pastel on handmade paper.

complicated forms are an ideal subject to help you improve your powers of observation.

Take time to analyse and understand a flower before you begin drawing it. Examine the bloom: what is its basic shape? Some flowers are bell-shaped or conical, others round. Try to think of a simple shape that best expresses that flower. Count the number of petals, stamens and pistils; observe the direction of the stem as it joins the flower. Measure the proportions of the bloom itself, its width and height, and compare them to the size of the leaves and the thickness of the stem. The shapes of the leaves and stems are just as individual as the flowers. It is a good idea to make little sketches of the leaves and stems to analyse their movement. Some flowers have hard, straight stems; others are flexible and curving.

Before you begin the painting, make sure that you have a clear picture in your mind of the shapes and proportions. To do this, make several little sketches, working these out before you begin. This will enable you to work at an even pace, observing the light and colour and trying to express the feeling and life of the blooms themselves.

A plant is a living thing; it moves, reaching up for the sun. The sunflower – a heliotrope – turns to face the east and follows the arc of the sun's life-giving rays until it sinks into the west.

We can see and appreciate the turn of a sunflower but the movement of the other plants are too slow for our eyes. Because they seem so static when we draw them, it is easy to forget their inherent movement. If this line of growth or movement is left out, an

The crisp, waxy texture of the lily was very attractive and called for very sharp, decisive drawing. A fairly smooth pastel paper was chosen to give clean lines, with a medium grey tone to contrast with the white petals. The drawing was done with pastel pencil and soft pastel.

Step 5 *At the final stage the leaves were blended to harmonize them, then the whole drawing was lightly sprayed with fixative before the details were drawn in. The fixative prevented the reds and yellows of the stamens mixing with the other colours. In order to achieve these rich colours, the edge of an orange and a red soft pastel were pressed into the paper with quite a force while the fixative was still fresh.*

The background was left plain, making use of the colour of the paper. Additional pastel would have interfered with the simplicity of the flowers by adding confusing texture.

Step 1 *To begin with, a simple outline drawing was made of the flower and leaves using a light pastel to provide a basic guide for the positions for the different parts of the flowers and to check the arrangement of the drawing.*

Step 2 *The cool colour of the leaves was put in next, to get a balance point for the tones of the drawing as a whole. The light petals are just indicated at this early stage to provide a note on their eventual position.*

Step 3 *A warm tone was added to the leaves and a dark tone of grey was drawn into the petals to give them a firm structure and shape.*

Step 4 *The flower began to emerge as very soft white pastel was used to draw the outline and highlights of the petals. Some of this white was blended inwards to make up the finished shape of the flower.*

important element in the drawing will be lost, and as a result it may resemble an artificial flower rather than a living one.

The Chinese and Japanese paint the stems and growth lines of a plant from the bottom or root upwards. They sometimes turn the paper upside down so the paint and line flows freely downwards, becoming thinner and lighter as it goes. When the drawing is righted, the stem has the perfect characteristics of thickness and weight at the bottom and a graceful sweep upwards.

PRACTICAL PROBLEMS

There are practical considerations to be taken into account when you are drawing flowers. Frequently the bloom begins to droop and turn colour as you are about to start working. When this is a problem, just lightly indicate the direction of the stem and move on to the blooms as quickly as possible.

Before starting work, prepare the flowers so that they will last as long as possible. Take off all the unwanted leaves and freshly cut the stems with a sharp knife or scissors. Crush the ends of woody stems to allow more water to enter. Then, if you have time, soak the flowers up to their necks in a bucket of water or tall container for a couple of hours before arranging them. You can use cut-plant food to extend the life of the flowers. If you are selecting flowers from a garden, cut them before the blooms have opened and been pollinated because once pollination has occurred the petals will drop off quickly.

CAPTURING COMPLICATED FORMS

Drawing the complicated forms of a rose, for example, is a challenge. The shapes of roses differ quite a bit. The specie rose, which is flat and open faced, gave an enduring image to English heraldry. This white rose, derived from the dog rose, was the favoured personal badge of Edward IV in the Wars of the Roses. During the 19th century, great, soft cabbage roses were developed that have wonderful, rounded forms. Try to find one of these roses in the bud and make a series of drawings as it opens, then of the flower in full bloom finishing with the petals beginning to fall. If you use a large sheet of paper, you can arrange all the studies of the flower to form a bouquet.

Step 1 *Because the flowers were fading and drooping very quickly the blossom was drawn in using the side of a soft pastel, starting with the light petals.*

Step 2 *Dark tones were added with yellow ochre for the petals on the far side of the flower. This clear separation of the two tones for the petals gives the drawing a feeling of depth.*

The sketch on these pages of the side view of a sunflower was done to get to know the flower before starting on the bouquet. The stems of a sunflower are strong and thick to hold the heavy flower as it turns. The movement and pale colour of the stems and leaves are very unusual. Three tones of yellow were used for the petals and all the colours were tried out on a piece of the same paper before the final colours were chosen. Always use a piece of the same paper or board as that which you intend to use for the final drawing, because trying out the colours on a piece of white or differently coloured paper would make their tones look quite different.

60

Step 3 *The stem and leaves were drawn using two tones of green. It is especially important to use a dark tone for modelling the form of the thick stem.*

PRACTICE

Collect as many different types of leaves as possible and make drawings of them. Observe their shapes and proportions and relative sizes, the different types of patterns formed by the veins, and the subtle variations in colouring.

Overleaf, a dark grey pastel board provided a dramatic contrast in tone to the flowers, and the surface allowed for fast work, so that each petal could be defined with one sweep of the pastel to demonstrate their extraordinary movement and shape. Pastel board has the additional advantage that it can hold thick layers of colour that resemble paint. By varying the pressure on the pastel stick you can change the mark from a subtle haze to the full intensity of the colour in a second.

The diameter of the centre of the flowers was measured in relation to the length of the petals before the drawing was started. This is a useful measurement to make with all open-faced flowers. In the case of the sunflower the diameter of the centre of the flower was twice the length of a petal – which was quite surprising.

Step 1 *A very pale grey Canson paper, which has quite a strong texture, was used. The blooms were drawn with a light blue pastel. A cool colour was laid down first in order to express the dim late-afternoon light and the fact that the flower's colour was fading.*

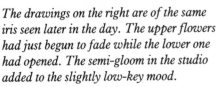

The bearded iris has a wonderful mix of colours from pink and mauve to copper. Soft pastel was used on pale grey pastel paper with a moderate grain as this will hold a thick, luxurious layer of soft pastel with enough depth to be pulled together and blended easily.

The drawings on the right are of the same iris seen later in the day. The upper flowers had just begun to fade while the lower one had opened. The semi-gloom in the studio added to the slightly low-key mood.

Step 2 *Deep tints of copper and red oxide were added to build up the petals. The movements of the petals were particularly interesting. As the upper petals opened, the lower ones slowly drooped, and the aim was to capture the difference between the opening bud and the fading flower.*

Step 3 *The colours are blended using a little finger to draw them together, to convey the sheen of the petals. The blending also gently pushed the pigment into the texture of the paper, creating smooth areas to contrast with the heavier texture in other parts of the drawing.*

Step 4 *Some detail and darker tones were added to the flowers, and finally the stems were drawn in. The need to finish the drawing quickly, before the light faded, meant that the flowers, which were very delicately lit by the light from a window, had to be done first.*

Step 5 *The background was gently layered, using soft pastels in two shades of blue. The background colours were then lightly dusted with a tissue to blend back the colours slightly in order to avoid a strong texture in the background, which would interfere with the main subject.*

A background should silently enhance a drawing, not overpower it.

When trying to capture the dying evening light on a subject, it is important to keep on working in natural light, even if it becomes quite dim. To turn on artificial lighting will completely destroy the mood.

The hybrid tea roses, which have a basic inverted cone shape, are graceful and easier to draw. If you look into the centre of an opening bud you will see the spiral of petals slowly unfolding. In certain hybrid tea roses the edges of the petals are ruffled, forming a frilly edge. Observe all of these points before even lifting a pastel because you want to be in possession of all the facts before you start drawing. It is important that the momentum of your drawing is as undisturbed as possible – hesitation always shows.

Try to block in as much of the drawing as you can, holding the stick at a sharp angle to the paper. You can use the full side of the pastel or part of the side, depending on the width of mark you need. Use the point or end of the pastel for details and lines. A pastel pencil is very useful for drawing thin stems and other fine details. The sharp edge of a delicate form can be drawn with a pastel pencil and then filled in, working away from the edge, with soft pastel. It is usually best to leave most of the blending to the end, but there are times when an area must be blended smooth before a detail or highlight is added over it.

Hard pastel sticks can be used on their own, or combined with soft pastel for a crisp effect, which may be more suitable for certain types of flowers than the more crumbly soft pastel. The type of paper you select is very important; pale flowers will stand out well against a tinted background. Generally, papers with a very strong texture are too harsh for the smooth and delicate forms of a flower. Pastel board or pastel paper work well and the new colours and tints are very attractive as a background. Artists' abrasive papers can be used successfully for drawing certain types of flowers, in particular dry varieties, but the ordinary abrasive papers from a hardware store are, in my experience, too coarse for floral subjects.

This rose was drawn in the late afternoon, with the last shafts of light touching the edge of the flower in such a way that the flower seemed to be illuminated from within. The basic shape was quickly blocked in with the side of a soft pastel, only using the point to draw the stem.

A very strong contrast was created by the choice of paper and by the light and dark tones on the flower. A strong 'jump' in tones always gives the impression of sharply defined light.

Drawing a bouquet of flowers is not too difficult if it is approached from the standpoint of composition first, flowers second. This doesn't mean that you should treat the flowers as mere geometric shapes – you still want to express the qualities of the blooms you have selected.

The basic shapes of the flowers and vase were drawn in with a light pastel. The vase was tackled next, and the stalks were drawn with heavy marks. The drawing was developed by adding the dark tones in the flowers, followed by the lighter tones. Then the leaves and deeper tones were built up. Highlights were added on the flowers to define them more clearly.

Textures

Pastels are really all about clear colour and varying textures. No other media can match the range of texture that can be achieved with pastel. No two drawings are ever alike; each one is a totally new discovery and experience, and by combining layers of colour or using thin blended areas under heavy textural marks you have dozens of ways to draw the same subject several times over. Besides the sheer fun of using texture, there is a more serious reason for its importance in pastel work.

Aside from using perspective, the pastel artist must use texture along with colour to create a sense of space and depth in the picture plane. Thin and smooth textures recede; heavy, dense textures appear to come forward. This effect is very simple and completely effective. A strong texture will also draw the eye to it and create a mood. However, too much texture of one type cancels out its own virtue. A heavily textured drawing begins to look like a woolly jumper, while a completely blended drawing becomes insipid.

Hitting a good balance isn't too difficult if you wait until the last stage of the drawing to do the blending. At this point, it is best to work very slowly, taking time to stand back from the easel to judge the effect of the blending. Try to create a contrast by offsetting smooth areas with heavy texture. The way you blend is also important. Use the side of your hand or the side of your little finger. A nasty, smudged effect occurs when you use the tips of your fingers, which are warm and moist. Many fresh, lively drawings have been lost by hasty over-blending, and once a drawing has become overworked, it is very difficult to bring it back. Having said this, there are of course cases where a background or another area must be blended smooth early on, before adding heavier colour or texture over it.

ROUGH TEXTURES

The whole technique of creating the right texture depends on the choice of paper and the pressure you use with the pastel stick, so select the type of surface that will suit your subject. A pastel can be pushed into the paper with such a force the mark will be completely solid, or it can be lightly floated over the paper, leaving a gossamer web of colour.

The type of pastel you use will also affect the drawing. If you are using the side of the pastel a harder pastel will not embed itself into the paper as readily as

A heavily textured paper was chosen so that it could be used to create texture on the rocks. It was also the same colour as the stones so that it would provide the basic colour of the rocks. Colour was worked around the rocks to bring them out. A warm black was used to put in the dark tones, picking up the texture of the paper. The grasses in front of the rocks were drawn with the sharp edge of a hard pastel to bring them out. The foliage and bushes in the background were kept as soft shapes to make them recede into the distance.

This great rock face had deep fissures running from top to bottom and had been honed over the millennia, providing an unusal opportunity to draw smooth rock faces. The colours ranged from cadmium orange on some surfaces, to a strange bluish hue, which shaded to deep indigo in the crevices. The whole spectacular design was offset by a curtain of heavy foliage. A pastel board was used and the colour was layered heavily. Once a sufficient amount of pastel had been built up, the colour was blended by pulling downwards across the paper to give the impression of the deep lines cut into the smooth stone.

a very soft pastel, so the hard pastel will leave less of a mark or trail on the paper. Soft pastel can be floated over an area of hard pastel successfully, but hard pastel only flattens and smears the soft pastel if it is used on top. With a very critical texture it is better to put the work behind glass as soon as possible and omit the fixative altogether.

Stones and rocks, with their varying surfaces, are perfect subjects with which to experiment with creating rough textures. Make the textures in your drawing strong from the outset as it is almost impossible to overdo a textured effect.

REFLECTIONS IN WATER

Images in water and glass are fascinating to draw. They are pictorial puzzles in which you draw the reality, and try to suggest its mirror image. As in all mirrors, the reflections are reversed and slightly darker than the original. In the case of, for example, trees reflected in water, you must take account of the verticals of the trunks intersected by the broken horizontal patterns of the water surface. If you sketch in this cruciform design lightly, you will have a basic shape for the drawing, which you can then begin to work up, tone on tone, to give an impression of depth in the watery foreground. Keep the tones in the foliage in the upper part of a drawing light as you will inevitably find that you have to deepen the water tones.

The colour of the water has to be taken into consideration as well. The reflections of trees in a muddy pond will be different to the same trees reflected in a clear stream. The shape of the distortions in the water will of course depend upon how calm the surface is. Generally the pattern of ripples on the surface diminishes in size as it recedes into the distance (see perspective, page 86).

DRAWING GLASS

The image seen through a glass or vase is dependent upon the shape of the glass. A curved surface will distort the image, moving it up or down and bending it along the curve. During the process of drawing, the image will change if your angle of view shifts, so to avoid confusion don't move around. Try to keep the same angle to the object. If the glass has water in it, the water can act as a lens, reflecting light and distorting the shapes of stems or other objects that are immersed in it. The best advice is to observe closely and draw exactly what you see, no matter how strange or distorted it may seem. When you step back from the easel, it will be convincing.

DRAWING IMAGES IN A MIRROR

There is a convention – or little trick – for painting convincing images in a mirror. As with other types of

A mirror reflection of the setting sun on a calm sea. The colours in the sea were put in with thick layers of soft pastel and blended to create the mirror-image effect.

Step 5 *Right, this is a critical part of a painting. The blending must be done properly to give the impression of reflection. Until now the colour has deliberately been left quite rough. It is best to do the blending at the end, using the side of a little finger. Place it on the area to be blended. Then, with a very firm pressure, pull and blend the colour downwards. All of the reflections must be done in exactly the same direction to produce the mirror effect. The tones were adjusted so that all the reflections in the water were slightly darker than the objects they were reflecting.*

Step 1 *The calm water in this village pool reflected the trees and houses like a polished mirror. First a light placement sketch was made using blue pastel and the darker tones were indicated with crosshatching. This was a very complicated subject that needed a strong structure of tones to make it work.*

Step 2 *The basic tones and cool colours were laid in with soft pastel. At this stage the drawing resembled an abstract painting, and was treated as such by turning the paper upside down to study the tonal structure. This type of drawing should be stood on its head several times before it is finished.*

Step 3 *Once the overall composition had been checked, more warm colour was added and some areas were lightly blended using the side of a hand.*

Step 4 *There was a dramatic change as the warm colours were put in. The intention was to build this drawing from a cool base of colour to tie together the water and shade, allowing the warm colours to flow on to the cool.*

reflections, an image in a mirror is reversed and slightly darkened. In addition, it should be drawn more softly, without hard edges. Strictly speaking, there are many times when a mirror reflection does match reality. However, when it is drawn less distinctly, a better illusion of a reflection is created. All mirrors have a certain base colour produced by the type and thickness of the glass. A thin, inexpensive mirror will be almost colourless, but a heavy plate-glass mirror will have a definite cool, blue-green cast.

BLENDING AND CREATING SMOOTH TEXTURES

For all of this work – whether water, glass or mirrors – you need to be able to create a very smooth surface with pastels. You might think a smooth texture is difficult to draw with pastel. Quite the contrary; it is actually easy.

There is one golden rule: use a good amount of soft pastel. Although it seems perverse, the more generous you are with the pastel, the better. Most new students start with a small area of thin pastel and with great effort manage to push it out to make a smooth but rather uneven texture. A thick layer of soft pastel slides over the surface like silk when you blend it.

You can put several colours on roughly with the side of the stick and blend them together with the side of your hand or finger. Don't put one on at a time. You will find it difficult to work additional colour into a blended surface effectively. If you must add another colour to a blended surface, remember to put on a generous amount so that you can blend it very gently to avoid smudging it in. The harder the pastel, the more difficult it is to blend. If you have an area of hard pastel that you want to blend, you can apply soft pastel in a similar colour over it and then merge it.

Abrasive papers cannot be used for blending. With pastel board you can move the colour a bit, but over a very limited area. Smoothly blended surfaces are better achieved on pastel paper or smooth-textured watercolour paper. The modern velour papers, which are copies of the real vellum used for portraiture in the 18th century, are sadly not comparable, giving nothing but a flat and overall smooth texture.

The acme of pastel drawing on this particular surface was the work of Jean-Baptiste Perroneau and Jean-Etienne Liotard. The latter spoke of his constant quest to set down as exactly as possible 'the smoothness of fine skin, the gloss and transparency of bodies, the colouring of flowers, the down and bloom of fruit'. Vellum allowed him to do so, for his work sometimes has the quality of fine china painting.

With a clear stream you are drawing not only the reflections, but also the rocks and other objects on the bed of the stream. The water will also appear to change colour as it rushes between the rocks and passes in and out of the shadows.

The shape of the smooth stones provided a good contrast to the movement of the water. The colours were put in roughly and the blending was done at the end, pulling the colour down the paper with a finger. Once the drawing was sprayed with fixative, a few lines of yellow ochre were added for the ripples.

The shape of the chapel was drawn in and the principal forms of the sky behind it were laid in with a good quantity of soft pastel. The sky was blended with the side of a hand, wiping across the whole area in a long sweep to blend the colours evenly to create a burnished effect. If the chapel had been drawn in first, it would have been impossible to get the evenness behind it. The ripples of the water were also added at this stage. As with the sky, the colour was laid in heavily, with a strong contrast, before being blended.

The chapel was drawn in last, together with the outline of the distant land, and the water was blended.

Sketchbook Work

If you hang up your camera and take a sketchbook on holiday instead, you will see and experience a place on a completely different level as you stop to give it the time and attention you need for a drawing.

There is one golden rule when you prepare to sketch out of doors: try not to be overladen. Plan a very compact sketching kit that you can always have with you, something that easily fits into a light bag. The exciting vistas always appear when you least expect them, and the weather suddenly improves when you have left a heavy kit at home.

For ease, a pastel pad is useful. If you want to try pastel board, cut it to the right size at home and tape it to a light piece of hardboard. Since the surface of pastel board disintegrates with the slightest amount of moisture, it is wise to put the board into a plastic bag for protection. Hard or medium-hard pastels are generally best for outdoor work. A small selection of different tones in hard pastels is very useful. Sketches

Right, the clouds were sweeping and stretching across this range of hills at sunset, and it was necessary to work very quickly. Several colours were used for the sky since the sun was reflecting differently off each layer. The large tree in the foreground helped to create a sense of space and depth in the picture.

Below left, a quick sketch using pastel pencil. Crosshatching is a good way to make a quick note of blocks of tone, and variations in the weight of line distinguishes nearer objects from those further away. Here, the heavy line and crosshatching on the rocks make them seem closer. The crosshatching and line were trailed off, using the lightest pressure on the pencil, for the fading effect of a distant plain.

Below, in this sketch of an old farmhouse a variety of marks were used to make a quick note of the different textures of the main elements in the scene. The spikey marks used for the leaves being blown across the face of the stone house create a sense of movement and life in the sketch.

of the landscape from the point of view of its tonal composition will give you a vital note on its structure. Combine this with a colour study and you will have the means to work out a larger composition at home. If you have time, make additional drawings of some of the details in your subject – a part of the architecture that may be difficult to remember, or the shape of a particular shrub or tree. The more information in your drawings, the better the finished work will be.

If you are not using a pad, some tracing paper is useful to cover the work when you have finished, and of course you will need fixative.

Carry a folding stool if possible, because the best view and the place to sit never coincide.

Don't try to do a finished work on a sketching trip. Use it instead to make several studies of the same scene, which you can then work up at home.

If you forget your sketching kit and come across something interesting, make notes of the colours. The sketch for the painting of Whitby Moors (page 87) was made with a biro on the back of an envelope. The

shapes of clouds and their movements were drawn, and crosshatching was used for the tones. A note was also made of the colours in the landscape. If you study colour, you should be able, after a little practice, to tell the difference between them. Your eyes will gradually be able to judge whether an object is indigo blue, French ultramarine, Prussian blue or cobalt blue. A note of indigo was made for the sky over the moors, and on a scale of 10 to 100 per cent of the chromatic value the deep colour in the sky was judged to be 80 per cent of pure indigo.

As well as noting colours and shapes, try to write down your feelings and impressions of the landscape; what it meant to you at that time. This is very helpful later on when you are working at home, and trying to get back into the mood.

Many people work very well outside, and prefer to do the finished work in situ. Others need the quiet concentration of a studio environment for the final work. You should work in whichever way you feel most comfortable.

Light

An indication of the light on the subject helps to create the illusion of reality and life in a painting. Light is an intangible quality that constantly changes, and when it is introduced into a picture it helps to fix the image in a moment in time. The viewer is aware that the landscape is being seen at a particular moment and that in a few minutes it will be different – the clouds will have moved or the sun and shadows will have shifted. It is not a static picture, but imitates life, giving it a special quality.

A glance at the sky to find and fix the direction of the sun is the first step in any outdoor painting. Good light is often poor light for a painter. A few rays of sunlight penetrating cloud cover, on the other hand, adds drama to an otherwise boring scene. One of the

Right, the overcast sky was setting in and the light was cooler than in the drawing below, due to the denser cloud cover.

Below, a vast panorama is one of the most difficult subjects in landscape painting. There is always the question of how much to use and how to organize it. The adverse weather conditions helped in this situation because the light and cloud effects gave a focus to the composition.

The study was done in a pastel sketchbook that had a linear pattern of waxy lines on the paper. It is quite curious and a bit difficult to work with, but in this case it worked well as it was possible to make a simple note of the storm slowly retreating across the peaks and to blend the colours to give the impression of sheets of rain scything down.

most important uses of light is to focus attention on one part of the picture, creating a strong centre of interest. This is often used in large panoramas, which are always difficult to compose. There is such a confusion of form and so many details in a vast landscape that it can become almost impossible to tie it together. If you can add light from a cloud formation to the composition, to illuminate part of the panorama, it will act as a cohesive force.

Light can also change the mood of a landscape, and indicate the time of year. A sharp contrast between light and shadow gives the effect of a bright summer's day. The more subtle the contrast, the softer the light will appear. Shadows are also an important part of a composition. They can add a sense of depth to a landscape and indicate the time of day and year. Long, low shadows, for example, suggest winter's gloom.

When you are working outside, your main concern will be to try to fix and hold on to a certain image of light that, by its very nature, is constantly moving across the landscape. Even on a clear day, the shift of the shadow patterns over the landscape in two hours is considerable. To cope with this, always make a note of the time of day on the corner of the paper so that you can come back to the subject if necessary at the same time the next day. In that way you can be sure that the direction of the light and the position of shadows will be the same when you return to a scene, although the quality of the light may have changed.

We are more sensitive to and knowledgeable about

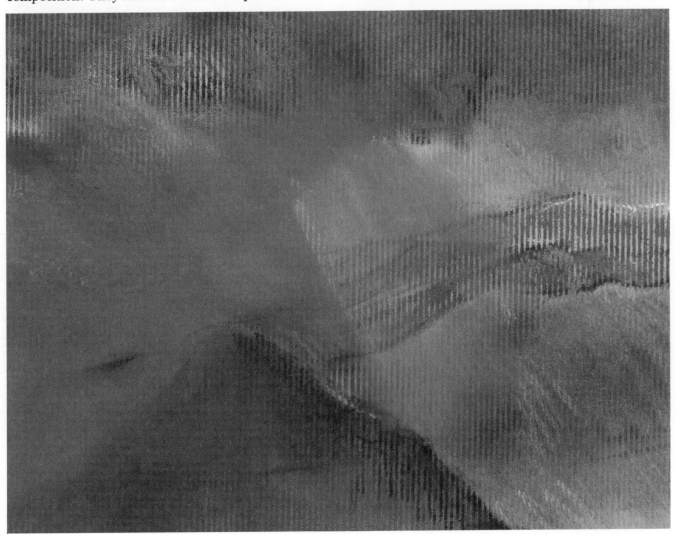

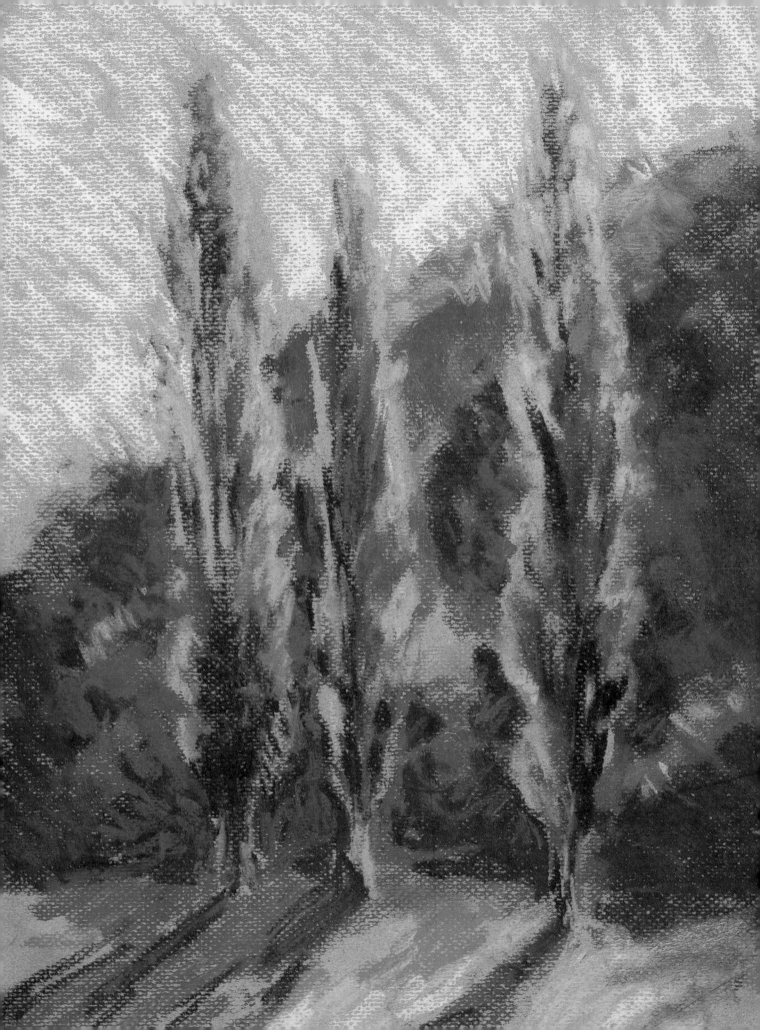

Above, sometimes the quality of the light is such that it can be the main subject of a painting. This early evening sky was done on a dark-toned paper. The paper was then moved on to a rougher surface and pink, orange and mauve were lightly floated over the sky. The surface underneath the paper gave the clouds a light texture.

Left, these poplar trees were catching the last warm light from the setting sun behind, which gave the leaves a halo as they shimmered in the evening breeze. The drawing was done very quickly. The dark centres of the trees were put in with a few strokes, followed by the illuminated edges in warm yellow. The shadows and hillside were put in with a cool blue. The long cast shadows were an important part of the contra luce *effect. No more blending or finishing was done as the sketch captured the immediacy of the moment.*

the differing qualities of light than we realize, and it is a powerful tool for creating both form and atmosphere in a subject. Claude Monet made a series of paintings that were carefully observed studies of the same haystacks at different times of the day and in different seasons of the year. They are a marvellous evocation of light and nature. You can see in his paintings how he used the colour of light to give a sense of cold in winter with a bluish tone, and summer's warmth with lemon yellows and orange tints. The colour of light at different times of day is also important. The setting sun can bathe a landscape or seascape in mauves and reds.

DRAWING LIGHT AND SHADOW

The conventional approach to this is to ask students to draw from a still life or model illuminated by a lamp or

The quality of light can create a mood. A dark-toned paper was rubbed over with warm greys and pinks. A sharp, cold blue and deep mauve were added and partially blended. The rough texture in these areas stands out and becomes the focus of attention in the composition. In the last stage of the drawing the horizon was darkened against the fading light.

PRACTICE

Choose some simple objects for a still life. A few pieces of fruit, some books and a bottle will give you a good selection of shapes and textures.

Place them on a table and use a lamp to the side to illuminate them. There can be a small amount of additional light in the room. This will give you a model of a landscape illuminated by the sun.

A few studies made of the play of light and shadow on the objects and the table will be a very valuable exercise for landscape work.

The lamp can be moved around the objects, and its height and angle altered, approximating the movement of the sun over the landscape.

spotlight. The problem with this approach, however, is that the student tends to draw the objects first, and then draws in the light or adds the shadow. This isn't, however, the way we see. The reverse is true; we notice the light on the object first, then we fill out the rest of the picture. This applies, of course, to well-lit subjects, not very subtle, modulated light.

In order to get back to that natural experience of light and shade, students should try to draw just the light they see on the figure or object, not the whole thing. Then do the reverse and draw just the shadows on the objects and the shadows that those objects are casting. In this way we can get a direct response to light quickly for its own sake. Later, of course, detailed drawings can be made to study the exact forms of the light as it curves around the forms.

Pastel is a wonderful medium for studying light. If you want to draw the light on a subject, use a light tone of soft pastel on a dark-tinted pastel paper or board. For the shadows, choose a light paper with a dark pastel. If you want to draw both the light and shadow, use a paper with a middle tone and try out your colours before you start, to see how well they will work on the paper you have chosen.

DO'S AND DON'TS

Do make a note of the direction of the light when you begin a drawing or painting.

Do make a note of the shadows if the light is changing.

Do use light or dark papers to contrast with the tones of your subject.

Do use light to focus on the centre of interest.

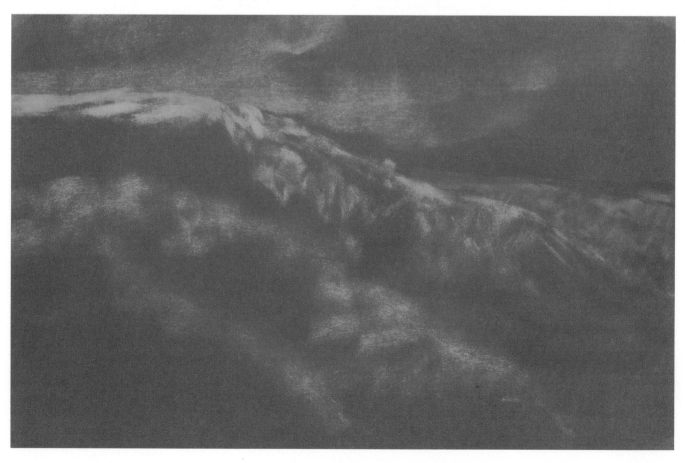

A study incorporating both light and shadows on the hills. In this moody, early-morning scene the hills seemed to be slumbering under a heavy blue mantle. As the sun slowly climbed in the sky the mantle dissolved, leaving the warm greens of trees and scrub. Because of the moving shadows the woods seemed to be flowing over the soft hills. First the hillside was drawn, framed by a window, following the rhythm of the shapes. The work was done quickly because the scene changed from moment to moment. The dark pastel board provided a good tone to work against and a very soft pastel was used on its side.

Left, even in a shorthand note such as this one of the light on the hills at sunset, the subject is recognizable. The variation in pressure used with the pastel, on a sensitive pastel board, created the variation in the depth of colour.

Space

Western artists have been obsessed with the problem of form and space for many centuries. It is curious how the East and West took different roads in art. Eastern artists concentrated their talents on creating exquisite designs and paintings on a flat plane, without making use of conventional perspective or lighting, completely accepting the two-dimensional surface of the picture for what it was. Western artists, on the other hand, sought to imitate natural vision with perspective and to create the illusion of light and shadow in their paintings. The two worlds came together with the importation from Japan of household china. The designs used on the wrapping paper were a revelation to the Impressionists, who managed to incorporate the clear colour and decorative quality of Eastern painting into the Western, naturalistic tradition. The effect of this union is still with us in the use of clearer design and colour.

However, the illusion of space and light still dominates Western art. For landscape painting it is important to understand a few rules of perspective. The eye level from which you are painting is the first consideration. If you hold up a pencil horizontally in front of your eyes, you will see that this line is exactly on the horizon. If you sit down, the horizon moves down with you to the level of your eyes.

Deciding where to put the horizon in a landscape painting is an important consideration. There is only one absolute rule, which is not to place it exactly half way up the page. There are few things as awkward as a landscape divided in half by the horizon. If you want to try some interesting variations on the usual placement of the horizon, take an idea from the Dutch landscape painters of the 17th century, such as Meindert Hobbema and Salomon van Ruysdael. They dropped the horizon line far down on their canvases to give space and importance to the immense cloud formations sweeping in from the North Sea. These paintings remain some of the finest landscapes ever created, although in one sense they are not landscapes as there is very little land in them.

Besides working with the horizon, there are other ways of creating space in a landscape, but they all have one thing in common – they make parts of the landscape recede into the distance. The same rules apply if you are drawing a still life or part of an

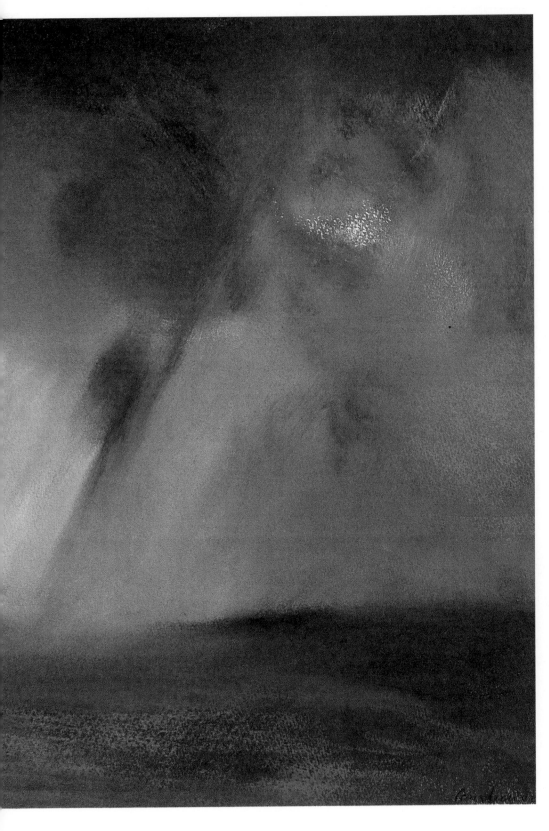

The north of England has some of the finest subjects for landscape painting, such as moorland with its autumn livery of deep purple heather. The play of light through rifts in the clouds can create a stunning effect, accentuating the warm tones of the heather and offsetting it against the subtle blues and greys of the receding moors. Here warm and cool colours have been used to create a sense of space through the use of warmer greens in the foreground and cool violet for the distant hills. Strong textural marks have been used for the storm cloud against the softer area of sky in the distance, creating a strong sense of space in the sky.

interior. In a landscape, architectural elements are drawn in perspective with either one vanishing point in the middle of the horizon or two points widely spaced apart. The lines of buildings are drawn to converge on these points.

Objects – trees, houses and so on – diminish in size as they recede into the distance. Artists frequently use this fact to create a feeling of great depth in a picture, drawing a tree or branch very large in close up in the foreground, with the rest of the landscape diminishing in size behind it.

Another way to make a scene appear to recede is to draw the subjects in the background less distinctly than the part nearest to you. The extent to which each part of the scene should recede depends upon your composition and the part of it that you want the viewer to focus on.

Our eyes focus like the lens of a camera on one area of vision at a time. If you are looking at a friend, his or her face will be in focus and the background of the room out of focus. You may not realize this at the time, for as soon as you look to see if this is the case, your eyes will focus on the background, and your friend will be out of focus. To make a drawing look real, artists try to copy the way our eyes work. To draw a convincing image, they deliberately focus on one area and soften or push back others. If we drew everything equally in focus, the drawing would appear to be without depth or space.

With pastel it is very easy to soften images. A slight amount of blending or blurring will push back a part of the drawing. Crosshatching or feathering also hold back areas and make objects less intrusive. As parts of a landscape recede in the distance, they appear lighter and cooler. Pale blues and mauves are generally used on distant hills or plains, for instance to achieve this in the distance. A smoother texture helps as well. You can use a tissue or a soft brush to smooth down a distant plane.

Conversely, warm tones and heavy texture will bring forward an area or object. With pastel the type of line or mark is also important. Try to lighten the pressure of the pastel on lines in the distance and make sure the area trails off.

You also need to draw objects to the right scale close up and in the distance, which is quite difficult as everyone has a tendency to underestimate the effects of perspective and draw distant objects far too large. You can measure and compare the sizes of objects in different parts of the scene to help with this.

Left, a cloud of smoke over a burning field was catching the evening light. Detail in the foreground and warm colours were used to bring some features forward, while other areas were blended back to make them recede into the distance.

Right, strong, bright colours have been used for the foreground foliage, and the building in the background has been suggested without too much detail.

Landscape

Landscape painting involves a marvellous communion with nature. In choosing a landscape to paint, you should react to your feeling of its rightness for you. This is a very personal thing – some people have a feeling for trees or water in close-up; others prefer long vistas of mountains or a rolling plain dotted with distant buildings. When you have found your subject, the first thing to do is to establish the source of light, and decide whether the light will stay reasonably constant. Then assess how the subject will work in terms of composition and colour. Ask yourself whether you can control the subject, marshalling its various elements into a satisfactory composition?

Another important factor with landscape is synthesis. It is vital not to allow yourself to be distracted by detail, and to reduce the motif to manageable proportions – even cutting out trees or buildings, if necessary, to make a harmonious design. The observable material should be the servant of your creativity, not its master.

Give your empathy with your subject matter its head. Don't become overwhelmed or bogged down by the preponderance of green, for instance. Let your pastel stick run with the light. The fussy detail of a

This bank of earth and heather was full of incredible colours, and the heather extended up the hillside. Soft pastels were used with a pastel pad. By blending back the earth and then redrawing with the same colour, it was possible to build up depth and weight. The dry heather was drawn with jagged lines and marks, with strong darks to balance and hold together all the bright colour in the composition.

Right, the sun was on the nearest hillside. The tones of the distant hills were darkened to emphasize the impression of light on the nearer ones. Each stroke of the pastel was used to define the directions of clouds or the planes of the hillsides.

This drawing is one of the clearest examples of the use of colour to build up shapes and form, instead of using it just to fill in shapes.

mass of foliage can become a fascinating design in various shades of green, yellow, ochre or even vermilion or indigo. This is where pastel can really display its versatility. Once you have blocked in the tonal mass lightly, have fun! Give yourself time to explore what is said to you by the interplay and harmony of light on trees, water or buildings, and experiment freely with colour. Paul Gauguin may have been indulging in special pleading, but he is reputed to have said, 'If you see a tree is brown, paint it red!' The clarity and purity of colour and the play of light are part of legitimate artistic licence.

You can be beguiled by a romantic and apparently manageable subject, only to find out that you have underestimated the complexity of it. It is best to try a small detail of a landscape to begin with. The large panorama is beautiful to look at, but a very difficult subject to organize into a painting. Some artists look through a small frame cut out of card until they find a suitable section of the landscape. The advantage of this approach is that you can exclude from your vision all but a small area, which can help you judge how it will work as a composition.

Never place your sketching stool very close to a

subject. Buildings, in particular, lose all scale that way. If you wish to sketch an interesting detail, say a group of houses, in receding planes, anchor them in the scene with strong foreground detail, such as a tree with strongly drawn diagonals of foliage to provide a frame. This leads the eye into the centre of the picture, the main detail of which should be kept light, its three-dimensional quality enhanced by the deep shadow over a door or a window frame. Provided the tones in the foreground are kept sufficiently strong, the

background will not intrude or look out of place.

The importance of light has already been stressed (page 78), but there are occasions, for example in the Mediterranean or in other regions with strong, constant sun, when you may find that towards midday the subject is 'whited out'. Unless you are relying on detail delineated by deep shadow, all tone dies. Some painters, British painters more than most, actually prefer fleeting light for a broad landscape, relying on capturing the mood of a moment. In the painting of

This noble lime tree was set against the deep chestnut wood. The light, mottled bark caught the light and appeared very solid and silvery.

Below, a shorthand note of the warm colours of autumn. The mauve and cold green set off the warm ochres and browns.

Whitby Moors (page 86), the 'searchlight' effect of the
sun penetrating through the clouds and sheets of rain
to illuminate only a part of the landscape underneath
has been caught with great effect.

Landscape painting can be very uncomfortable,
particularly when you are in the depths of the country.
The clouds of flies develop a frenzy, making
concentration well-nigh impossible. The next time you
admire a particularly free passage in a drawing or a
painting, enlivened with a flick or two of raw colour,
consider that it might well be that the artist was
running before the local insect life!

WORKING OUT OF DOORS
Pastel is a quick medium to use, which is a great help
for landscape work. Here are a few practical tips that
may help.

A pastel pad is a better choice for working out of
doors than loose paper. Remember to take along some
masking tape to hold down the corners of the pad in a
wind and fixative for spraying the work when you
finish. Make a note of the time of day on the corner of
the paper so that you will find the light in the same
direction if you return to finish the drawing on another
day.

There is an advantage to using tinted paper for
open-air work. The tinted paper gives you a basic tone
that holds the composition together. It is the same
principle as body colour in painting, where the darker
tones are put on a middle ground for structure and the
lighter tones are then added for highlighting. With
this simple technique you can make a quick note of the
landscape, and you always need to work quickly. The
sun and the weather take no 20-minute breaks of pose
while you refine your thoughts on the subject and
rearrange and clean your materials for another stab at a
particularly intractible clump of trees, reflections in a
pool, or gathering stormclouds over a mountain.

Out of doors the light is changing all the time,

*Skies such as this tend to change in a very short space of time,
and it is vital to work quickly in such conditions. Concentrate on
what is really important – here, the quality of the light in this
dramatic mountain landscape. All areas have been treated very
simply, with no attempt to put in any detail.*

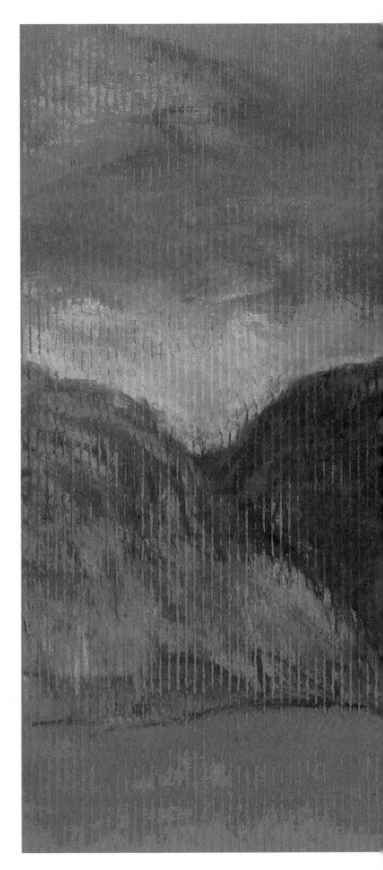

DO'S AND DON'TS

Do try a simple landscape first, before tackling a large panorama.

Do explore fully the range of colours and textures in areas of foliage.

Don't let yourself be distracted by details, however interesting they are.

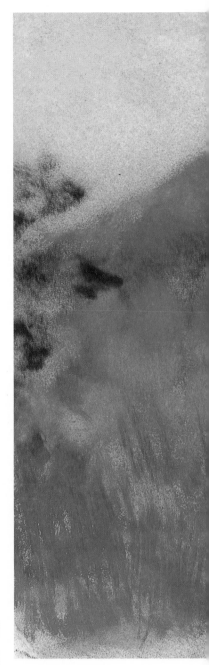

Right, an experiment with strong colours on a pastel board. The effect of working with such colour on a semi-abrasive board is very intense. The afternoon light turned the mountain a warm russet colour and the heather added to the indigo shadows that spread up the slopes. There was a problem: the rich colours on the mountain were making it come forward, not recede, in the drawing. Normally the distance would be created by using pale mauves or blues on the mountain to push it back. Instead, sharp, dark tones were added in the foreground to pull it away from the mountain and thus create space.

Step 1 *The mountains in the distance were just indicated with pale grey.*

Step 2 *The row of trees was blended back and lightened to make it recede into the distance. Textures and details were added in the foreground, while the mountain was left light and simple.*

dancing over the subject like a will o'the wisp, and before you know it, it can disappear, leaving what was a lively, three-dimensional form full of colour and vibrancy as a flat monotone. To cope with this, make a point of drawing in the placement of the light in the landscape as soon as possible. A light crosshatching for the shadows is a good method of placing them, and an arrow for the direction of the sunlight will give you a reference as you continue to work. Then, if the weather changes, you can work from your memory of the light and from your marks on the paper.

The artist may seek storm effects – J. M. W. Turner, after all, had himself tied to the mast of a fishing smack to observe a storm at sea – but it is always better to try to catch the lowering majesty of the advancing weather front rather than to allow yourself to be caught right in the middle of it.

It is no accident that most Impressionist paintings with a landscape subject matter preserve a sense of eternal high summer in the Seine valley or the

Step 1 – *The main shapes in the composition were drawn in first, including the directions of the clouds in the sky, and a note was made of the dark area in the foreground in case the weather conditions changed.*

Step 2 – *Colour was built up throughout the composition, with strong, dark colours being used in the foreground areas. Lighter colours were used in the distant part of the scene, applied with angular marks to create the jagged quality of the mountains.*

Left, the evening storm was racing across the landscape and engulfing the top of distant hills. Full rein was given to the movement in the landscape, and the colours in the sky were layered before being blended together. They were blended by sweeping a hand across the pastel board to create soft edges, taking care not to lose the sharp patches of light on the horizon. The two dominant colours are the complementary pair, blue and orange – in this case dark blue and brown, which is the darkest tone of orange.

Step 3 – *Stronger, warmer colours were added in the foreground to make it appear to advance. Cool blue was added in the distant sky, and cooler greens were added in the landscape. The colours in the distance were blended back increasingly as they recede into the distance.*

PRACTICE

Try using the Impressionists' colours in a landscape. Use bright, clear colours on a piece of small abrasive paper or a pastel board. Remember to vary the tones of the colours by using deep colours as well as light ones. The abrasive paper will help you achieve a rich, painterly effect. Keep the drawing very simple and use flat, unblended colour. The Impressionists used blues or mauves in the shadows and heightened the colours they observed. If a tree had brown bark they might paint it red. The greens were clear and the lighter colours were frequently lemon yellow and pale pink.

Normandy coast. The Impressionists summered there, working outdoors as often as the weather allowed, and then decamped to their studios in Paris to work up the sketches they had made or sell the finished canvases – if they could. The Post-Impressionists, and particularly the Fauvists, required strong light for their work with its vibrant, heightened tones, and they therefore moved south for the better part of the year.

Two of the first artists to use the vibrant impasto of pastel for landscape sketches were Eugène Delacroix and Eugène Boudin. The poet Charles Baudelaire said that visiting the latter's studio was to be overwhelmed by the forces of nature, so powerful were the sketches covering the walls, depicting the play of light on the sea in various weather conditions.

Sky and Weather

Although a bright sunny day is a welcome treat for the artist working out of doors, it is not necessarily best for a landscape painting. An empty sky is boring, it lacks movement and does nothing to create a sense of space; nor does it provide a frame for the landscape. Worse still, a blank, light sky provides no balance to the scene below. Nor does it finish; it just seems to drift ever upwards out of the picture frame.

As you would expect, artists have devised a number of subtle techniques to deal with this problem. One method is to darken the uppermost part of the sky very slightly and gradually, providing a lid that helps to contain and settle the composition. You can see this device in use in some of the Impressionists' work. In fact, a sky is never totally flat and uniform; there is always a lighter area, its position depending on the time of day. At midday, the lightest part will be overhead, while at sunrise or sunset the light will be close to the horizon line.

The best skies to draw are those with some interesting cloud formations, which give drama and movement to landscape. They also enhance the composition by giving the picture a three-dimensional quality.

Step 2 *The sea was blended to contrast with the texture of the cloud, and several tones were added to the sky to create the impression of depth. All of the drawing was kept as loose as possible to maintain the feeling of space, air and, above all, movement.*

Step 1 *A sky study using only tone, in order to examine the structure and forms more closely. It is always a good idea to try out your selection of tones before starting, to see how they work together – is there enough, or too much contrast between them?*

The basic shape of the sea and cloud were drawn in on a grey-tinted pastel paper.

Step 3 *A cold blue was added to the sky for further depth, giving a strong contrast in both tone and texture. Once the cloud had been blended the drawing was sprayed with fixative and then a soft white pastel was lightly floated over the sky to pick up the light on the tips of the clouds. A pale chrome green was used for the softer area near the sea.*

One key factor in drawing cloud effects is to observe and note the angle or direction of the clouds in relation to the horizon line. Contrary to general belief, few clouds run parallel to the horizon. Most are moving at an angle to it. This is a great help to your drawing, because it creates a clear sense of depth in the picture. The clouds lead the eye into the landscape and opposite the straight horizon line. The most interesting formations run at a sharp diagonal to the horizon, giving the picture energy and drama. The diagonal lines are caused by strong winds at high altitudes pulling the clouds against the denser atmosphere at lower levels and the air resistance of the landscape itself. Frequently clouds are moving at very different speeds, and this is visible to the artist. The effect is more apparent when you look at clouds passing over mountains.

Several types of clouds may be in the same sky at the

same time. We know from flying in bad weather that clouds are not all thin and fluffy, but contain tremendous amounts of energy. For example, on a hot, humid day the cumulus are being lifted by a thrusting wave of expanding warm air. If you are in an aeroplane, you can see the cloud churning and boiling as it expands upwards to the freezing level of the stratosphere. Once the cloud reaches this level it 'anvils out', forming the familiar flat, anvil shape at

This was drawn quickly to catch the movement and energy of the boiling clouds over the mountains. The contrast in textures helps to define the developing thunderhead.

Step 1 *These clouds were drawn on light grey pastel paper, and dark grey was used for the base colour. It was put in very roughly and then blended.*

Stage 2 *A second layer of soft white and light blue pastel was added and left unblended to give the clouds movement and depth.*

PRACTICE

Prepare and keep a notebook with sketches of
different clouds and weather conditions. Try to
find a book on meteorology at your library to
study. Make careful sketches of the different
cloud formations in pencil and write down the
names of the types so that you can easily
recognize them. Later you can use these to make
further studies on dark pastel paper with soft
pastels. These notes and drawings can be used as
reference material to enhance and add interest to
dull landscapes that need some shape and form in
the sky. Practise controlling the pressure on the
pastel to create both the light textures and the
density of the clouds.

*The clouds sweeping across the hills were bringing bad weather,
and the angle of the side of the hill was used against the sharp
angle of the clouds moving over it. The two diagonal lines of hill
and cloud made a strong design and composition. The texture of
the hill was left untouched to contrast with the blended texture of
the cloud.*

Step 1 *The clouds were reflected in a mirror image on the sea. A quick note of the shapes was made in a simple blue tone.*

Step 2 *The clouds were moving, stretching out over a calm sea, and the main aim was to draw this movement very quickly as the sun was setting, the shapes and colours changing every few moments.*

Step 3 *Right, the colours of the sea were blended by pulling them down vertically with the side of a finger. No additional colour was added to the sea; the effect was achieved by letting the colours mix as they were blended together.*

top. Observe the clouds before you begin your work; a drawing should try to express the energy and movement as well as the shape. A good way to begin is to make a quick note of the lines of movement in the sky. A few lines will do, or better still use the side of a pastel to rough in the sweep of the clouds. Remember that they will be changing as you work, so speed is essential.

The colour of clouds is dependent on two factors. The first is the amount of moisture they hold, their density. The heavier the cloud, the darker it should appear in the drawing. The clouds are also affected by light from the sun being reflected back by features such as expanses of water or dust in the atmosphere. A calm sea acts as a mirror, reflecting the warm light and colour of the sun on to the clouds at sunset and sunrise. High winds can pick up dust and sand from the earth, turning the sky a bright orange.

Above, a quick note of a cumulus nimbus moving across the landscape. This was made as tonal study of the forms.

Above right, a tonal study of the clouds sweeping across the hills.

Right, this glorious mountain and sky were drawn in a few minutes, capturing perfectly the brooding atmosphere of the scene.

Overleaf, an early summer
morning. The sun seemed to
stain the hilltops a blood red
and turn the sky salmon pink,
except where the receding dusk
left layers of indigo and ice-
blue.

Assessing Your Work

In his old age the great Japanese artist, Hokusai, believed that if he had been granted another five years he would have mastered his art. To anyone familiar with his work he had passed the point of mastery decades earlier. Nonetheless, he felt it had not been achieved. Picasso was never totally satisfied with any of his paintings. Total perfection in art is a mirage, always slightly out of reach.

It is fairly important to assess your work – with the emphasis on fairly. Many worthwhile paintings are torn up in frustration, their good points overlooked because of some mistake that can easily be corrected. The advantage of pastel is that it is a very forgiving medium; changes can be made without damage to the basic fabric or texture of the paper.

First you must find out what is wrong. The ability to assess your work objectively is absolutely vital to its development. It isn't a matter of just having a good look at it. After working on a drawing or painting for a couple of hours you become too close to it, and you need to stand back from the work – both physically and mentally – in order to look at it with fresh eyes. There are a few methods that can help this process.

The drawing above was done on the spot. Studied later in the studio, the drawing needed greater depth. Right, the mountain in the distance was pushed back by adding a light layer of blue and grey. The foreground was broken up and brought forward with a grove of light beech trees, which were in the wood but not in that position.

CHECKING THE TONAL STRUCTURE

Regardless of your subject matter your work needs a coherent tonal structure. This is usually the basic trouble with most paintings. To check the tones, turn your work upside down and stand a good distance away from it. By turning it upside down the drawing element of the work is eliminated, and you can concentrate on the composition. Ask yourself if the work has a good dark, middle and light tone. The problem may be that it has too many mid tones and lacks the contrasts of very light or dark tones.

A 'black mirror' is a useful tool for checking the tones of a drawing. You can make a black mirror very simply by painting one side of a piece of glass with flat black paint or by taping black card to the back of the glass. For safety, put heavy tape along the edges of the glass. Hold the mirror so that it reflects the painting. The black tone of the glass neutralizes the colour and converts the work into a tonal composition, making the assessment much easier.

If the tones of the colours need to be adjusted make the changes in the mid tones. See which ones can be darkened to pull the composition together. Remember that the centre of interest in the composition can be strengthened by giving it a strong contrast in tones. If you think your work lacks a light tone you may need to spray the work with fixative before adding highlights or a light colour.

Left, a black background can be a very effective way of showing off a delicate flower. The strength of the background forces you to work with aplomb and daring, and the change of pace can be very helpful to your work in general. In a sense the tables – or tones – are reversed, because you must pull out light from a dark paper instead of tackling the usual problem of adding dark tones to a light background.

Above right, experiment with different coloured backgrounds in order to move your work on.

CHECKING THE COLOURS

After checking the tones take a look at the colour balance. A frequent problem with pastels is 'chalking out', that is, you may have used colours that contain too much white. Try adding a few clear colours. The amount of colour you need to enliven the work may be very little. Work slowly to avoid unsettling the complete composition.

Check for complementary colours in the work as they can help. Usually a painting has one dominant set of complementary colours, along with the other colours. It may be a work where either red and green, yellow and mauve or blue and orange predominate. If there is no complementary contrast in your work the colours may look a bit lifeless.

MAKING CHANGES

Never throw away a work unless you understand what is wrong with it. If you let the problem pass, you will only have to face it again in another painting. One tears up a work, but not the mistake. That can only be avoided by understanding it. Mistakes are usually not trivial slips of the pastel but some problem or weakness in observation or composition.

When you have worked out what is wrong, use fresh bread for any erasure to avoid damaging the texture of the paper. Don't be afraid of making a mess; it is more important to work out the mistake. Once you have done this, you can tear the painting into a hundred pieces if you want to.

If a drawing needs more radical treatment, use a wash of clear water on it. This will help to unify the existing work and you can then draw over it with a line when it has dried out a bit. Unfortunately the wash will only work on heavy paper.

DEVELOPING YOUR WORK

Experiments with a few radical changes in the way you work are exciting and can also be a help in its development. The easiest way to change your work is

115

to experiment with different types of paper or boards. Since pastel painting is so dependent on the type of surface you choose, even a slight variation in paper will need a change in technique. If you have been working on pastel paper you could try using a heavy watercolour paper or pastel board. The change in texture will take some getting used to, so give the experiment enough time. A strong background colour is another challenge. You can use any type of coloured paper so long as it has enough tooth to hold the pastel. Drawing on a black background with either soft or hard pastel is a very different experience again. Try leaving some of the black paper showing through the drawing for an attractive half-tone effect.

This huge old plane tree had a smooth trunk with subtle colours on the bark and a heavy umbrella of leaves. The soft colours and solid form of the trunk were fascinating and were the focus of the drawing.

A very dark shadow was drawn down two-thirds of the trunk to give it a strong, solid mass. The same strong shadow was put in up among the branches. Several light tones were scumbled together on the left side of the tree.

The house which was sketched in the background was too intrusive so it was pushed back by crosshatching with a soft mauve pastel. This had the advantages of creating depth and simplifying the picture. The mauve tint also helped the colour balance, providing the complement to the pale yellow tones in the tree trunk.

Above right, back view of a ewe drawn with a pastel pencil.

Right, hard pastel was used on a pastel pad to draw this ewe. The fine lines are caused by the texture of the paper. The patio was in shade, and was darkened even more to give a sharp definition to the animal.

If you are used to soft colours, change to primary colours for a few drawings. When you go back to your normal way of working, your colour sense should be heightened by the experience. Or try the opposite, using black and white with minimum colour for a few drawings. New working practices have to be carried on for several drawings, or at least a couple of weeks, to have any effect because it takes quite a while to get into a new technique.

Index

A

Abrasive paper 14, 15, 20, 21, 49, 56, 66, 74, 99
  erasures 19
Animals 117
Assessing your work 112–17
Asymmetry 35, 40
Atmosphere *see* Mood

B

Background 28, 31, 65
  and tonal structure 33
  black 114, 116
  coloured 21, 56, 115, 116
Binder 11, 14, 16
Black mirror 114
Blending 8, 10, 13, 15, 17, 42, 65, 68, 72, 75, 88, 98
  direct 44
  for smooth texture 74
  visual 44–9
Blending tools 20–1
Blocking in 66
Bockingford cartridge paper 19
Boudin, Eugène 99
Bouquets 67
Bread, as eraser 19, 115
Buildings 88, 92

C

Canson paper 64
Canvas 18
Cardboard 18
Carriera, Resalba 8
Cartridge paper 14, 19
Centre of interest 34–5, 55
  positioning 35, 40
  using light 79, 84
  using tone 28, 114
Chalking out 22, 31, 115
Charcoal 19
  as base layer 44, 45
Chardin, J.-B.-S. 8

Classical composition 38
Cleaning pastels 16
Clouds 54–5, 86–7, 100–8
  angle of 102
  colour of 108
Colour(s) 22–33, 90
  and depth 88, 96, 99
  and form 90
  and tonal values 28–33
  checking 115
  complementary 24–7, 31, 98, 115
  distinguishing 77
  Impressionists' 99
  limiting 31
  memorizing 23
  mixing 43–4
  selecting 22–3
  strong 96–7
  trying out 60
  warm and cool 23–4, 87
Colour study 77
Coloured backgrounds 21, 56, 115
Coloured paper 18, 19, 20, 31, 33, 49, 58, 116
Combining pastel types 14
Complementary colours 24–7, 31, 98, 115
Composition 34–41, 66, 90
  and tone 28, 33
  in still life 35–8
  sky 100
Conté crayons 14, 19
Contrast
  light and shadow 79
  of shapes 35
  of textures 68
  of tones 28, 33
Cool colours 23
Corrections 19, 112, 115
Crosshatching 14, 35, 42, 49, 72, 76, 88, 116
Curves 35

D

Damp paper 10–11, 14
Dark colours 33
  paper 16, 20, 84
De la Tour, Maurice Quentin 8

Degas, Edgar 8, 19, 38–40
Delacroix, Eugène 8, 99
Depth, sense of 36
  skies 102, 104
  using colour 88, 96, 99, 112
  using shadow 79
  using texture 68
  using tone 100
Detail 10, 66
Developing your work 115–16
Diagonals 35, 102, 105
Disharmony 24, 35, 40
Distance, sense of 36–7
Distortion, water and glass 70
Drawing, tonal 30
Dusting with tissue 65

E

Erasures 19, 115

F

Fabriano papers 19, 20, 21
Fauvists 27, 99
Feathering 45, 49, 88
Fine work 14
Fixative 14, 16, 58, 77, 94
  spraying between layers 45
  spraying technique 21
  with watercolour effect 11
Floating 17
Flowers 6–7, 10–11, 15, 18–24, 44, 56–67, 114–15
  preparing 60
  stems 60–1
Foliage, colour 91, 96
Form
  creating with light 81
  defining 8, 32
Framing 41, 91
Frottage 50–3
Fruit 17, 25, 42, 49

G

Gelatin solution 21
Glass, drawing 70
Grey 30
  warm and cool 28, 31
Gum tragacite 14, 16

H

Hair spray 21
Hand-made pastels 17
Hanemuhle Ingres paper 19
Hard pastels 14–16, 17, 42, 49, 66, 76
Horizon, placement of 86

I

Impressionistic approach 10
Impressionists 26, 86, 97–9, 100
Ingres paper 19
Iris 10–11, 21, 57, 64–5

J

Japanese art 6, 60, 86

K

Kneaded eraser 19

L

Landscape 12–13, 23, 24, 26–31, 34, 36, 90–9, 112–13
  creating space 86–7
  light effects 78–81, 85

panoramas 78–9, 91
perspective 86
(*see also* Outdoor work)
Large soft pastels 17
Layering 8–10, 16, 17, 43, 68, 69
hard with soft pastel 69
Leaves 61
Leonardo da Vinci 8
Light 65, 66, 78–85, 90, 92–4
and shadow 79, 81–5, 86
direction of 40, 84, 97
drawing 81–4
outdoor work 79, 94–7
Light coloured paper 84
Lily 6–7, 58–9
Line drawing 10, 14, 42, 66
Liotard, Jean–Etienne 8, 74

M

Marks 16, 48
Masking tape 19, 94
Materials 14–21
Measurement 56–8, 61
Mirror reflections 70–4
Mixing colours 43–4
Modelling 14
Monet, Claude 81
Mood, and light 81–2, 92
Movement 55, 58, 76
clouds 100, 103–4, 106, 108

N

Notebook 77, 84, 105
Nu pastels, *see* Hard pastels

O

Observation 58, 66
Outdoor work 14, 76–7, 94–9
light conditions 79, 94–7
Over-drawing 19, 20, 31

P

Paper 14, 18, 19–20
experimenting with 116
flattened 14, 19
for blending 74
for flower pictures 66
for frottage 52–3
for texture 68
Pastel board 14, 18, 20, 61, 66, 74, 116
for sketching kit 76
Pastel drawing 11
Pastel pad 76, 94
Pastel paper 14, 19–20, 66, 74
Pastel pencils 6, 14, 15, 48, 49, 66, 76
sharpening 14, 15
Peony 18
Permanency 188
Perréal, Jean 8
Perronneau, J.-B. 8, 74
Perspective 70, 86–8
Pigments 14, 18, 22
Planning 14
Pointillism 46–8, 49
Portraiture 23
Pressure
and texture 68
varying 16, 42, 48, 61, 85
Primary colours 23, 117
Putty eraser 19

R

Reflections
in mirrors 70–4
in water 12–13, 70–5, 106
Rembrandt pastels 16
Rocks *see* Stones and rocks
Romantic composition 38–40
Roses 18, 20, 60, 66
Rough textures 68–9
Rubbing back 10

S

Schmincke soft pastels 16
Scumbling 43, 44–5, 116
Seascapes 54–5, 70–1, 100–1, 106–7
Sennelier soft pastels 16, 17
Seurat, Georges 49
Shadow
and colour 26
and light 79, 81–5
drawing 81–4, 97, 116
Shapes
defining 10
diversifying 35, 40
Side of pastel, using 42, 49
and texture 68–9
Sketch 11, 58
tonal 30–3, 77, 100, 108
Sketchbook 40, 76–7
Sketching kit, outdoor 76–7, 94
Skies 54–5, 70–1, 75, 78–9, 81–3, 86–7, 94–5, 100–11
empty 100
Smooth textures 74
Soft pastels 16
for blending 74
technique 43
Solid colour 13
Space, sense of 31, 32, 35, 37, 38, 55, 86–9
using colour 88, 96
using texture 68
Spraying 21
Still life 24
composition 35–8
creating space 86
light and shade exercise 82
Stones and rocks
frottage 50, 52
textural effect 68–9
Storm effects 97–8
Strong colour 96–7
Sunflower 60–3
Sunlight 78
Supports 14, 18
Symmetry 35
Synthesis 90

T

Textural effects 8, 10, 17, 38, 68–75, 76
rough 68–9, 82
smooth 74
(*see also* Frottage)
Textured paper 19, 68, 78, 116
Thistles 15
Tinted paper 14, 20, 53, 66
for outdoor work 94
Tintoretto, Jacopo 8
Tonal compositions 28–31
Tonal structure 28, 33, 72
checking 33, 114
sketching 30–3, 77
Tone 13, 48
and colour 28–33
Torchon 21
Tracing paper 77
Trees 30, 32, 35, 48, 51–3, 80, 92–3, 116
Turner, J. M. W. 97

UV

Unblended marks 8, 13
Unison pastels 17
Vanishing point 88
Vellum 74
Velour papers 74

W

Warm colours 22, 23–4
Washes
coloured 20
water 11, 14, 115
Water, reflections in 12–13, 70–5
Watercolour effect 11, 14
Watercolour paper 10–11, 20, 74
Weather 78, 100–11
Wisteria 56
Wood-pulp paper 18

Useful Addresses

R. K. Burt & Co. Ltd
57 Union Street
London SE1
Distributors of Fabriano paper and
Hahnemuhle Bugra paper.

ColArt UK
Whitefriars Avenue
Harrow
Middlesex HA3 5RH
Distributors of Conté pastels.

David W. Ford
Cosmos Brushes
400, Beacon Ridge Lane
Lafayette
CA 94596
USA
Distributors of Schmincke pastels
in the USA.

Frisk Products Ltd
7-11 Franthorne Way
Randlesdown Road
London SE6 3BT
Distributors of Rembrandt pastels
and Frisk pastel board

MICADOR Australia PTY Ltd
20 Clarice Road
Box Hill
Victoria 3128
Australia
Distributors of Schmincke pastels
in Australia.

C. Roberson & Co.
1A Hercules Street
London N7 6AT
Distributors of Schmincke pastels
in the UK.

Taker S.A.
Provenza 31
E-Barcelona – 29
Spain
Distributors of Schmincke pastels
in Spain.

Tollit & Harvey Ltd
1C Lyon Way
Rockware Estate
Greenford
Middlesex UB6 0BN
Distributors of Sennelier pastels,
Goldline papers.

Unison Pastels
Thorneyburn
Tarset
Northumberland NE48 1NA

Acknowledgements

My first acknowledgement must be to my long-
suffering husband, John Crossland, who
sustained the creative effort needed to produce
60 drawings on a very tight deadline while in the
depths of the Cevennes National Park, South-
Western France.

I would like to thank our dear friend, the painter
Oliver Gollancz, for the generous use of his
Cevennes studio, and also the French National
Tourist Board in London and P & O Car Ferries
(on their Portsmouth-Bilbao route) which helped
us to arrive stress free at France's back door.

Diana Constance